CW01188213

First published in 2023
by Suddenly Publishing
22 Sheaf Street, Daventry,
Northants, NN11 4AB, UK

Editor: Joanna Clements
Publishing Director: Cheryl Thallon
Photographer: Mark McGuire, Big Adventure Media
Design: Kaye Smith

Text copyright: Oliver McCabe, 2023
Design copyright: Suddenly Publishing, 2023

All rights reserved. No part of the publication may be copied or reproduced without the prior written consent of the copyright owner.

A CIP catalogue record of this book is available from the British Library

ISBN: 9781739342418

Kids' Kitchen Takeover

Healthy Recipes & Fun Food Skills
By Wholefood Chef **Oliver McCabe**

Suddenly Publishing Ltd.

Contents

Introduction

8. Hello!
9. My Mission
10. Eating Well
12. Fruit and Vegetables
14. Water
16. Tips for Keeping Healthy
17. Nutritional Knowledge
18. Local Health Stores
20. Safety First
21. Let's Cook!

The Recipes

22. Good Morning Porridge
24. Berry Mango Soaked Oats
28. Homemade Oat Cream (Egg Replacer)
30. Easy-Breezy Pancakes
34. Sweet and Spiced Granola
38. Stewed Apple and Rhubarb
40. Oatylicious Bread
44. The Family Bread

A Delicious Feast!

48. Smoothies
50. Everyday Veggie Stock
52. Hearty Veggie Soup
54. Spice Up Hummus
56. Baba Ganoush Hummus
60. Basil Sunflower Pesto
62. Tamari Toasted Seeds
64. Sundried Tomato Falafel
66. Super Power Veggie Croquettes
70. Tasty Sundried Tomato Sauce
72. Veggie Meatballs
76. Chickpea Coconut Lentil Dahl
78. Sweet Potato Beanie Burgers
82. Rockin' Ratatouille Quinoa
86. Nutty Veggie Noodles
90. Vegtastic Pizza
94. Mama's Mashed Potatoes
96. Wren Cottage Veggie Pie
100. Rocket and Pear Salad
102. Creamy Lasagne
106. Lemon and Ginger Muffins
110. Cashew Lemon Icing
112. Choco Apple Banana Bites
116. Fluffy Flapjacks
120. Nana's Fruit Tea Slice
123. Cacao Hot Chocolate

Healthy Living

33. Breakfast
37. Food Storage
43. Meal Planning
47. Cleaning Up
69. Lunchbox Recipes
75. Staple Foods
85. Teenage Kicks
89. Eating Together
93. Parties and Picnics
119. Sports Activities
124. Nutritional Information
134. About the Author
136. Acknowledgements
138. Further Resources

That's Me!

Hello!

I'm Oliver, the wholefood chef, and this is my first cookbook created especially for kids!

This cookbook is plant-based, which means that I use fruit and vegetables and wholefoods such as grains, beans and cereals.

It's full of nutritious and easy recipes for you to make in your kitchen with your family. I have included recipes that you can use for breakfast, lunch, dinner and snacks – eat them for whatever meal suits you best and don't be scared to make them your own by swapping ingredients and trying new flavours. It's all about sharing the experience and making these recipes together. Cherish these recipes and they will support you on your onward journey. Maybe one day you will be teaching your own kids how to cook your favourite recipes.

Thank you for investing your time and effort into this cookbook. There are many fun recipes for you to cook as well as helpful skills to learn with lots of interesting food facts and easy nutrition advice.

Have fun!

Oliver 😊

My Mission

Do you want to be able to run faster, think smarter, have better skin and hair, and feel stronger? The source of these youthful superpowers can largely be found in the food and drink we consume daily.

More importantly, perhaps, what kind of grown-up would you prefer to be? Healthy and active or unhealthy and ill? Food and lifestyle habits have a big part to play in our immediate and distant future.

Food choices affect mood too - the right nutrients or lack of them can impact on whether you feel confident, happy and energised, or sad, anxious and tired.

Making bad choices repeatedly over time often leads to illness, low energy and low mood. We know that even a few days of eating junk food makes us feel sluggish, but also that the reverse is true – eat well for a week and you start to feel fabulous! Making good food and lifestyle decisions can make the world of difference.

Don't panic! It's ok to eat junk food occasionally, just don't have it every day. Use this cookbook to discover new healthy dishes which taste great and will help you eat a wide range of different foods. To help guide you, keep a list of all the individual foods you eat for a week – apple, banana, burger, cheese, bread (count each type of food only once). Try to eat as many as you can, 50 different foods is a good aim. Ideally, at least two-thirds of what you eat will be natural wholefoods – fruits, vegetables and grains that haven't been mixed with any other ingredients like sugars or additives. The recipes in this book are a great start to get you on your way.

Your health and happiness is in your hands. Forget about what you ate yesterday – your new relationship with food starts here.

Make yourself comfortable in your kitchen, get familiar with some new ingredients, take over the cooking for a few days a week. You'll be amazed and delighted at how much fun you have and how much better you feel! You might even find your family and friends want to join in.

Start a health and happiness revolution in your home by staging a kids' kitchen takeover – your body will thank you!

Eating Well

When we cook, we decide what is going into our bodies to nourish ourselves.
Between ages 4 and 13 your body and brain grow rapidly, so it is really important to make sure you get the right nutrients you need to build a strong foundation for the rest of your life.

Growth spurts and rapid cognitive development means there is a huge demand for healthy nutrients to fuel your body. B vitamins become increasingly important to ensure you have enough energy for your day. Vitamin B5 can be especially helpful for mental performance and focus and you can find this in foods such as mushrooms, avocados, nuts and seeds. Magnesium is important too. Involved in over 300 reactions in the body, it can even help to encourage good sleep!

Omega 3 fats are needed for both brain development and vision. Great sources of Omega 3 include walnuts, flax seeds and kidney beans. Alternatively, you can take vegan omega oils to help boost your intake. Healthy vision also relies on vitamin A. An effective way to ensure you are getting enough vitamin A is through eating green, yellow and orange vegetables which are rich in beta-carotene, or by taking a children's multivitamin and mineral supplement.

Strong bones are supported by calcium and vitamin D. Foods like kale, broccoli and lentils are good plant-based sources of calcium. The same foods will also provide iron – an essential nutrient for day-to-day energy levels and also for long-term growth and cognitive development.

Having adequate amounts of good quality protein is vital for growth and repair of tissues so make sure they include pulses and nuts and seeds. The last three are vital to focus on if they are vegetarian or vegan so include a good mix and add in plenty of wholegrains too.

11

Fruit and Vegetables

Visit your local independent health store, greengrocer, grocer or farmers market to source the best selection of fresh fruit and vegetables. They can be found in an ambient section (on shelves in the store or outside of the store) and also can be found in the chilled section of the store (refrigerated).

Ask the shopkeeper or member of staff any questions you may have on fruit and vegetables such as "what's in season"? "Where can I find a certain ingredient in the store?" or "Do you have any local fruit and vegetables in stock currently?".

Always visually check fresh fruit and vegetables for any signs of damage such as bruises, discolouration, mould, slime or leaking fluids. Do this whilst shopping not when you get home.

Always smell fresh fruit and vegetables for any unpleasant odour, particularly in the summertime as fresh produce is more at risk of being perishable with hot temperatures speeding up decomposition.

On the next page you can see where to find and store fruit and vegetables.

PRODUCE	AMBIENT	CHILLED	FROZEN
Fresh blueberries	●	●	
Fresh lemons	●		
Fresh cherry tomatoes	●	●	
Fresh bananas	●		
Fresh pineapples	●		
Frozen mango			●
Fresh avocado	●		
Fresh limes	●		
Fresh apples & cooking apples	●		
Fresh carrots	●	●	
Fresh baby spinach		●	
Fresh potatoes	●		
Fresh parsnips	●	●	
Fresh onions	●		
Fresh celery	●	●	
Fresh sweet potatoes	●		
Fresh courgettes	●	●	
Fresh garlic	●		
Fresh red and green chillis	●		
Fresh coriander leaves		●	
Potted coriander	●		
Fresh peppers	●	●	
Fresh ginger	●		
Canned sweetcorn	●		
Frozen sweetcorn			●
Fresh broccoli		●	
Fresh aubergines	●	●	
Frozen petit pois			●
Fresh brown or white mushrooms		●	

Water

Water keeps your body working properly. It makes up two-thirds of the human body and does lots of important jobs. Your blood contains a lot of water which enables it to carry oxygen to all the cells in your body. You need water to digest your food and get rid of waste. Water is also in your lymph – a fluid that is part of your immune system that works to fight off illnesses. Water also helps to keep your temperature normal. So it is really important that you top up your water tank to keep you in good health!

Aim to drink 4 to 6 glasses of water every day to fuel yourself adequately. If you have done lots of sports or it is a hot day, be sure to drink extra water.

Top Tips for Staying Hydrated

- Pack a water bottle for school and when you go out.
- Try taking a frozen water bottle out with you in the summer to keep it cooler for longer.
- Remember to have a drink before and after sports.
- Try adding slices of fruit to water for added flavour.
- Drink water with meals and snacks.

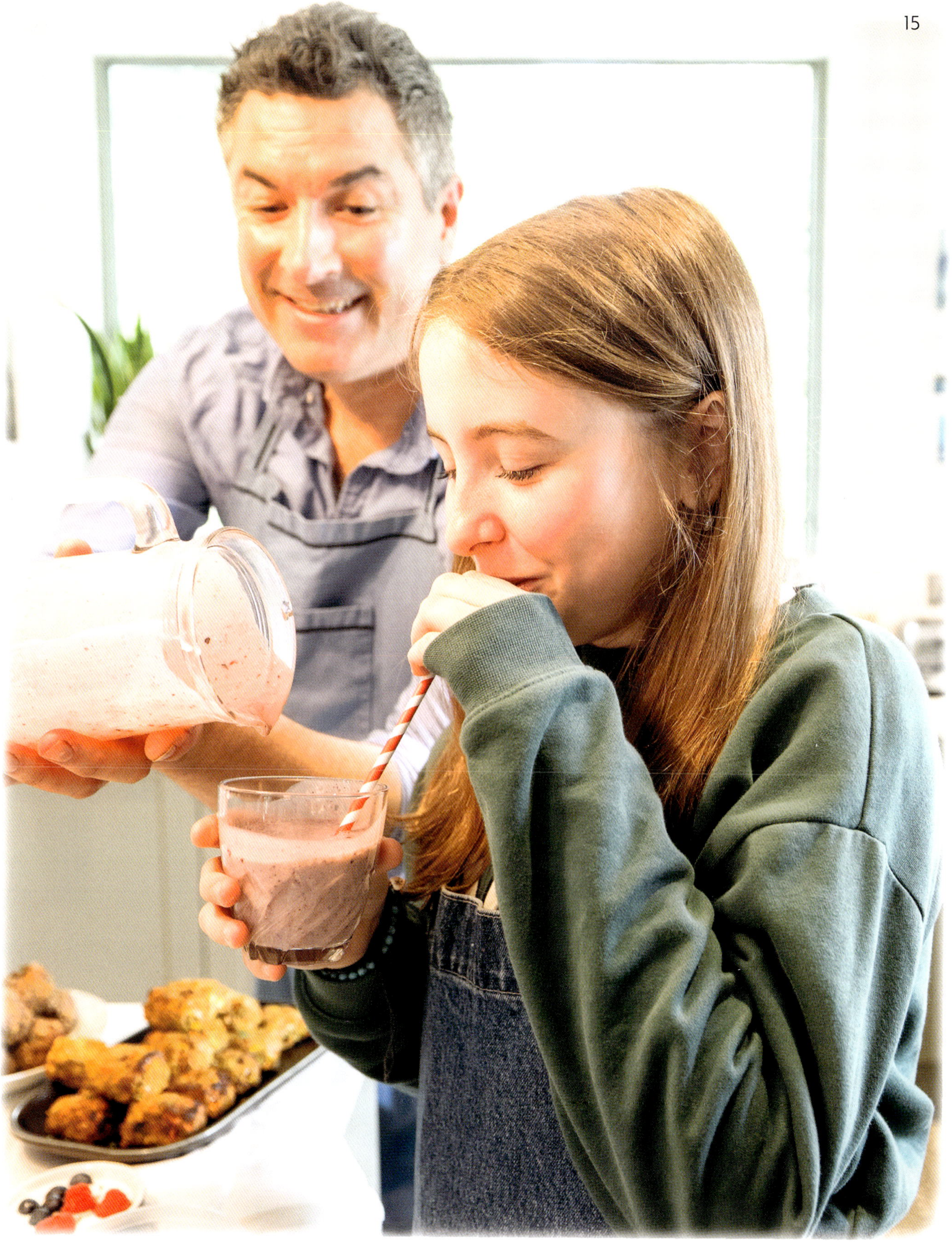

Tips For Keeping Healthy

1. **Eat Right**
A nutrient-dense diet is essential for your overall health and development. Aim for at least 5 portions of colourful fruit and vegetables a day and try to vary them each day. Incorporate calcium-rich foods, healthy fats and wholegrains and avoid too many sugary foods.

2. **Stay Fit**
Just 60 minutes of active play or sports every day is so good for your mental and physical wellbeing. If there's an activity you particularly enjoy have a look for a local club or get your friends to join in with you!

3. **Sleep Well**
Your brain and body need 8-12 hours of sleep every night for recovery and growth. It's always best to get into a routine of going to bed at the same time every night and try to avoid screens for at least an hour before bedtime.

Nutritional Knowledge

Carbohydrates, protein, fats and fibre are known as 'macronutrients' because we need them in large amounts in our diets. These nutrients fuel our bodies and help keep us well when we eat the right balance.

Carbohydrates

The main nutrient that fuels the body is carbohydrates. The more 'whole' the carbohydrate is - such as whole wheat, whole grain, quinoa and millet - the longer the fuel will last. Carbohydrates can be found in all types of grains such as brown rice, wheat and oats as well as products made from grains including pasta, bread and crackers, starch vegetables such as potatoes, peas, beans and corn, all fruits and their juices and plant-based milks.

Protein

Protein is needed for your growth and healing, energy and vitality, mood and behaviour, performance and recovery, a healthy immune system and good digestion. Eating 2 to 3 servings of plant protein is an adequate amount per day. An easy way to remember the correct serving size for protein is by the size of the palm of your hand. Your needs reflect your size. Foods with an excellent source of plant protein include beans, lentils, quinoa, seeds and millet.

Fats

Healthy fats are important to help us feel fuller for longer and they help aid a long list of essential functions in our body. When eaten in large quantities, especially before sports activities, fats can make you feel heavy and slow down your digestion, making it difficult for you to use as fuel. The good fats found in olive oil, coconut oil, nuts, seeds and avocados are essential fats for daily bodily functions.

Fibre

When we eat dietary fibre from the food we eat we are creating a flow inside our bodies which keeps our digestive system healthy and maintained efficiently. We obtain fibre from whole grains, milled seeds, fruit and vegetables.

Local Health Stores

Have you been to your local health food store lately? With thousands of different healthy products to choose from, they can be a one-stop shop for everything natural, organic, ethical and environmental.

Health food stores come in all shapes and sizes: unique, passionate and individual, just like us. The beauty of independent shops is that they are free to give you all the time and attention you need.

For the staff in independent health food stores, their priority is to help people become as healthy as possible, by combining an extensive range of specialist skills, foods, products, therapies and services to create powerful tools for wellness.

There are more than 1,000 independent health stores across the UK and Ireland; they are on the local high street, online and at the end of a phone - offering call and collect, delivery and in-person services customised to your needs. Get advice on lifestyle adjustments to support you for an active, healthy future.

Find your nearest independent health food store on findahealthstore.com

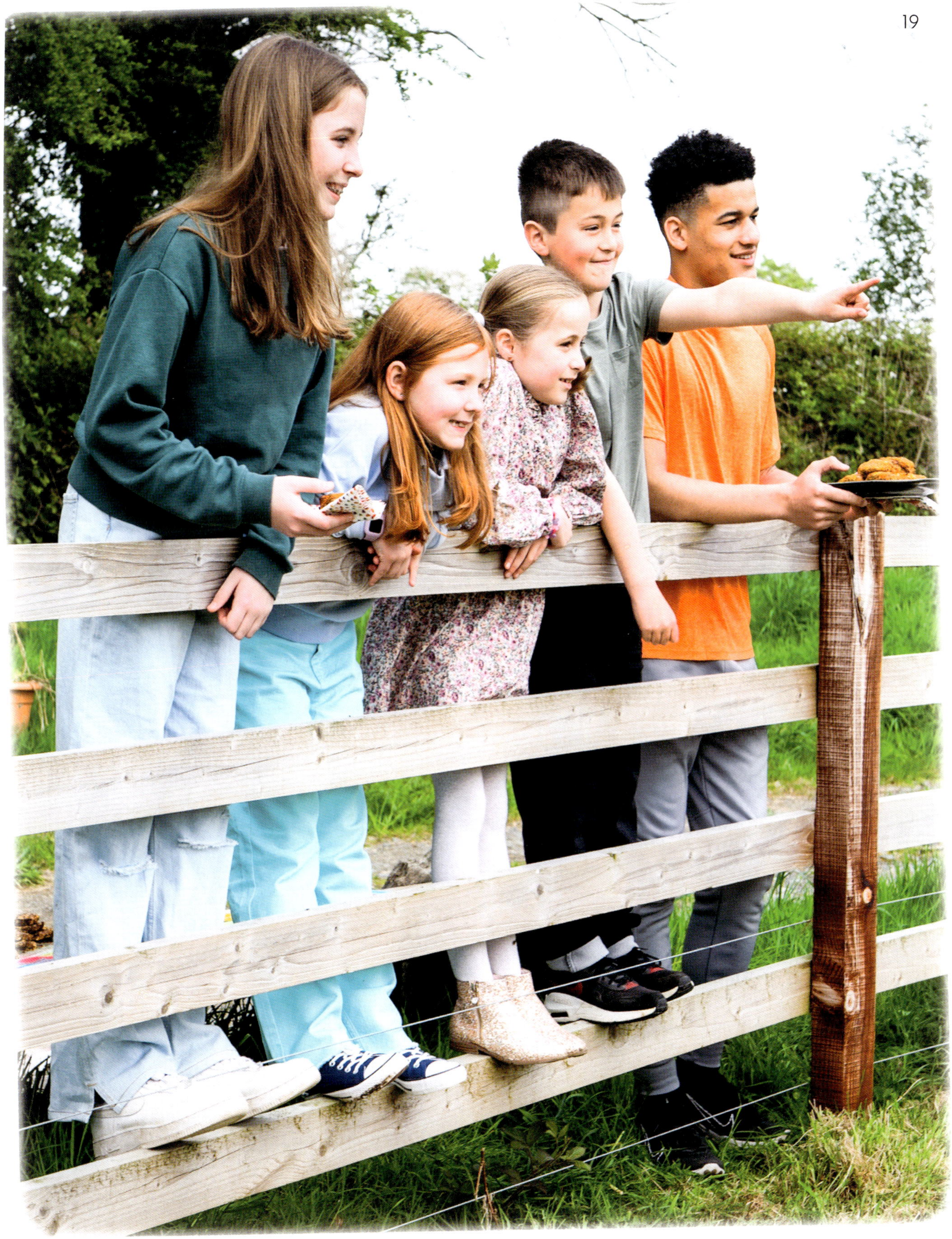

Safety first

Use oven gloves where the recipe informs you.

Take care when using knives, never point a knife at anyone.

Make sure your chopping board is clean, and not sliding on the kitchen surface.
If it is slipping, put a damp teatowel below the board to steady it.

Never touch electrical items, plugs or switches with wet hands.
Make sure electrical items are completely switched off before cleaning them.

Keep electrical appliances away from water.

Wipe up spills straight away, especially on the floor.

Don't use sharp knives unless supervised by an adult. Use a dinner knife with this cookbook for chopping or slicing, it's much safer.

Remember the stove/hob in the kitchen can stay hot for a long time after it is turned off.

Always, make sure all handles on pots and pans are turned inward.
This ensures that the handles can't be knocked or grabbed.

Pot and pan handles are hot whilst cooking so always have a small dishcloth or potholder ready to grip handles safely during cooking. Ask an adult to assist if required.

When removing a hot pan from the stove to an appropriate heat-resistant surface let everyone know in the kitchen by saying loud and proud – "HOT PAN COMING THROUGH!". The same is to be said if you are removing a baking tray from the oven to an appropriate surface.

Always turn off the stove, hob and oven when you are done cooking.

Never leave anything on the stove unattended.

Put ingredients back where you found them after using them to make clean up easier.

Cleaning up after yourself is part of the routine. Make it fun, turn the radio on and put everything away efficiently with some music.

Wash your hands thoroughly again with hot water and hand sanitiser before leaving the kitchen and dry your hands thoroughly.

Let's cook!

Before you start...

Wash your hands thoroughly with hot water and antibacterial hand wash.

Dry your hands with a towel until all of your hands are dry.
(Repeat this process during preparing recipes as well).

Put your apron on with pride!

Read the recipe through carefully, and collect the kitchen equipment, pans, utensils and ingredients.
(Ask for support from an adult if required).

Follow the recipe carefully, step by step, and follow the images throughout the recipe to assist you.

Clean up after yourself and leave the kitchen as you found it, so the next family member can cook the same as you.

Be considerate and leave the kitchen smiling!

Good Morning Porridge

Serves 2

I feel it is important to provide an easy oat porridge recipe to start your day, especially for the beginning of the new school term and during the autumn and winter months. This will certainly put a jump in your step, it is pure warming soulful breakfast food to keep you going throughout your day. You can add whatever fresh fruit or topping you like on your porridge. My favourite is simply sliced banana with maple syrup, I love fresh blueberries too with some shelled hemp seeds. Yum! So please create your favourite cooked porridge with whatever makes you happy. This recipe is best eaten straight away.

You'll Need:
- Small saucepan
- Measuring jug
- Wooden spoon

Ingredients:
- 50g oat flakes
- 125ml plant-based milk
- 125ml water
- 1 tsp maple syrup
- 1 tsp sesame seeds
- 1 tsp desiccated coconut
- 1 tsp raw coconut oil

Topping suggestions:
- Maple syrup
- Yoghurt
- Seeds or nuts
- Fresh fruit – blueberries, banana, apple etc.

Timing
Prepping: 5 mins
Cooking: 5 mins

1. Add the oats to a small saucepan with the plane-based milk and water. Place the saucepan on a medium heat stirring occasionally with a wooden spoon for 3 minutes until the oats expand and fluff up.

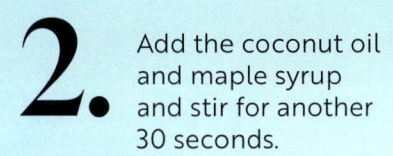

2. Add the coconut oil and maple syrup and stir for another 30 seconds.

3. Add the seeds and desiccated coconut, lower the heat and stir for a further minute until it is creamy. Spoon into breakfast bowls accompanied with your favourite toppings.

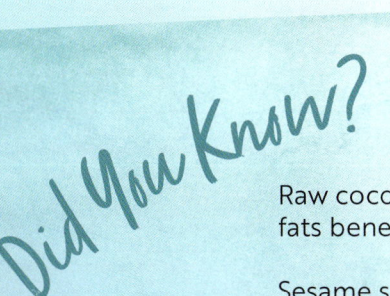

Did You Know?

Raw coconut oil is rich in MCTs, essential fats beneficial for our overall health.

Sesame seeds are a good source of B vitamins beneficial for our nervous system.

Berry Mango Soaked Oats

Serves 5

Timing
Prepping: 10 mins
Soak: 4 hours

A summer alternative to porridge is fruit-soaked oats. It is also delicious for a fruity wholefood snack or dessert. Soaking is best done overnight, however about 4 hours should be enough to soften the oats and make them tasty. This dish will keep for up to 3 days covered in the refrigerator. A few heaped spoons of the soaked oats in a small breakfast bowl should be a suitable portion.

You'll Need:
- Chopping board
- Knife
- Blender
- Measuring jug
- Medium sized mixing bowl
- Resealable food-grade container
- Citrus juicer
- Grater
- Wooden spoon

Ingredients:
- 1 lemon
- 600ml plant-based milk
- 250g fresh mixed berries (e.g. strawberry, blueberry, raspberry)
- 200g frozen mango
- 2 tbsp maple syrup
- 250g oat flakes
- 100g grated pear (or apple)
- 2 tbsp desiccated coconut
- 1 tbsp shelled hemp seeds

1. Cut the lemon in half and squeeze the juice with a citrus juicer out of both halves. Add the plant-based milk, berries, mango, lemon juice and maple syrup to a blender jug and blend for 10 seconds.

2. Place the oats in a medium-sized bowl or airtight container. Add the blender mixture to the oats and stir together with a wooden spoon.

3. Add the pear, coconut and seeds and mix well with a wooden spoon, making sure all the oats are coated and there is no dryness left.

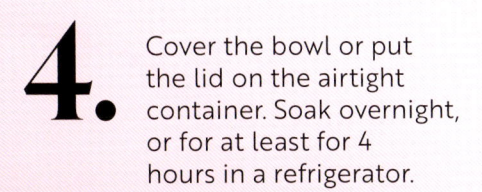

4. Cover the bowl or put the lid on the airtight container. Soak overnight, or for at least for 4 hours in a refrigerator.

5. When the time is right, spoon into serving bowls and top with your favourite berries and a scattering of seeds.
This will keep for up to 3 days in the refrigerator in a resealable food-grade container.

Heard This?

Lemon juice is a natural preservative which can preserve the food it's added to, such as this soaked-oats recipe.

Berries are a good source of antioxidants vital for maintaining good health.

How Did You Make It Yours?

Adding your own twist is a great way of making a recipe yours. Give it your own name and list anything you did differently!

My Recipe Notes

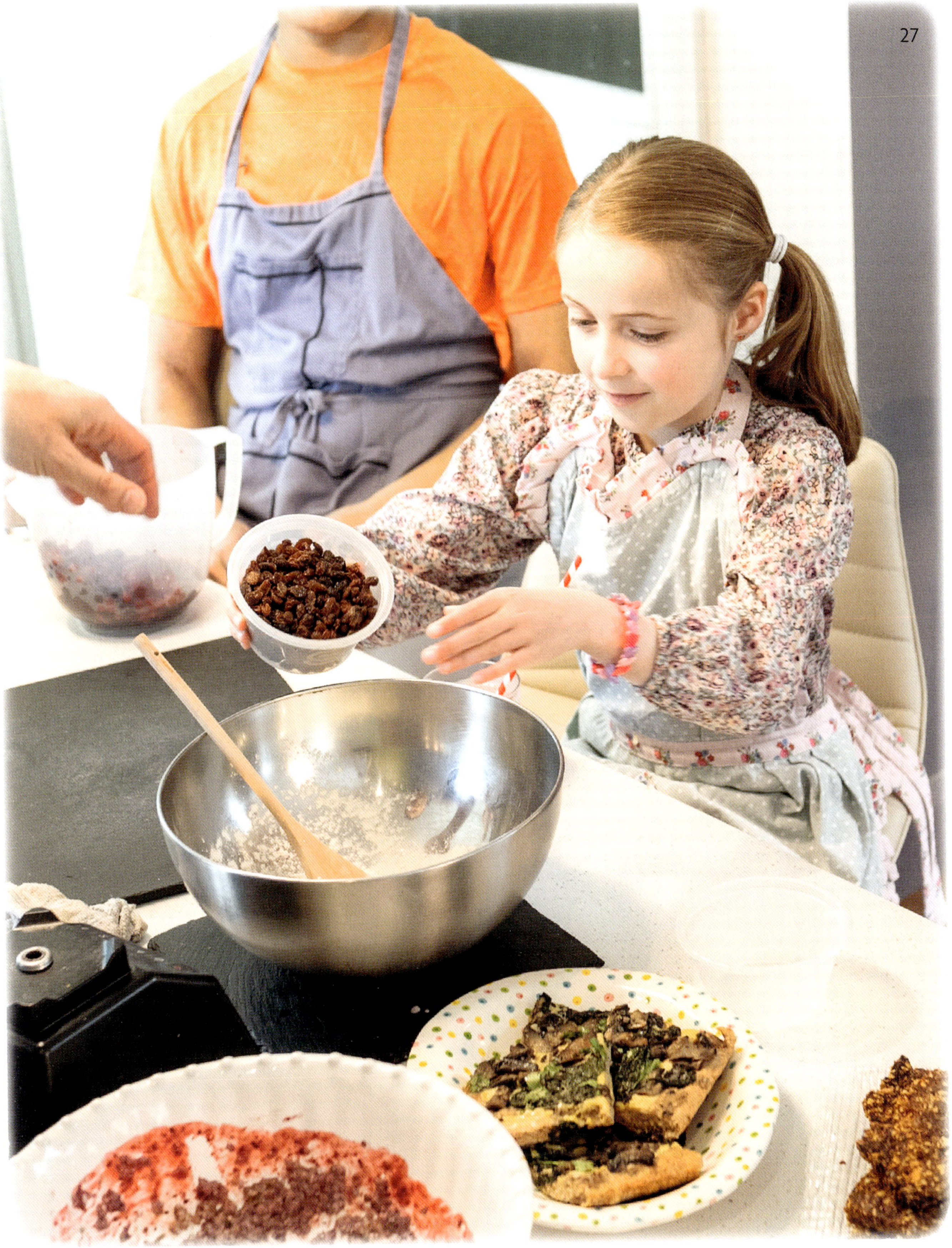

Homemade Oat Cream

Check it Out!

Oats are a good source of calcium and magnesium which helps to strenghen your bones.

Himalayan salt is found in the glacier salt deposits of the Himalayan Mountains in Asia.

Makes 700ml

This easy essential recipe was invented for this cookbook as an egg replacer. It can be used throughout the cookbook in various recipes and works very well and keeps up to 3 days in the refrigerator. I go through quite a lot of it so I always have some pre-prepared for various dishes throughout the week. It's very economical and a good source of fibre from the oats.

You'll Need:
- Blender
- Measuring jug
- Resealable food-grade container

Ingredients:
- 150g oat flakes
- 1 pinch fine salt (Himalayan is great)
- 1 tbsp extra virgin olive oil
- ½ tsp baking powder
- 300ml plant-based milk
- 300ml water

Timing
Prepping: 5 mins
Soak: 7 hours

1. Soak the oat flakes with the rest of the ingredients in a sealed container in the refrigerator overnight or for 7 hours at least.

2. After soaking, place the mixture in a blender and blitz until smooth. Pour into a resealable food-grade container to use for later. Keep in the refrigerator for up to 3 days.

29

Easy-Breezy Pancakes

Makes 6-7 Medium Pancakes

Pancakes have become an everyday breakfast, lunch or dinner staple. Just make sure to prepare your Homemade Oat Cream the night before. If you've forgotten, you can use egg replacer. They are so fun and easy to make, you can eat them for any meal. Once plated, sprinkle your favourite sliced fruit or dried fruit on top, or perhaps add some seeds and extra maple syrup if you wish. Or you can roll them with a delicious filling inside such as peanut butter and sliced banana. The pancake batter can be kept in the refrigerator in a sealed container for up to 3 days.

Timing
Prepping: 6 mins
Cooking: 6 mins

You'll Need:
- Blender
- Chopping board
- Small knife or dinner knife
- Citrus juicer
- Measuring jug
- Medium frying pan
- Spatula

Ingredients:
- 150g plain or self-raising flour
- 150ml homemade oat cream (see page 28 for recipe) the equivalent of 2 medium eggs
- 3 tsp xylitol
- 2 tsp maple syrup
- 1 tbsp raw coconut oil
- 1 tsp baking powder
- 150ml plant-based milk
- 1 lemon

1. Place all the ingredients (except for the lemon) into the blender. Cut the lemon in half and squeeze the juice from both halves into the jug.

2. Blend all ingredients for 15 seconds.

3. Add some coconut oil to a medium frying pan on a medium heat. Once it's hot and the coconut oil has melted, pour enough mixture into the pan to create a medium disc-shaped pancake.

4. When the pancake bubbles after a minute or two, flip your pancake with a spatula and fry the other side.

5. Fry for 1 minute and flip again if you wish, have fun!

6. Then place the pancake on a plate, repeat these steps if you want more pancakes. Sweeten your pancake naturally with some maple syrup and fresh fruit on the side.

Deeeee-licious!

Nuggets of Knowledge!

Xylitol is a plant-based natural sugar found in many fruit and vegetables.

Maple syrup is a good source of vitamin B2 and manganese supporting the metabolism of protein, carbs and fat within your body.

Breakfast

Getting up in the mornings is much easier when you have a good breakfast to enjoy!

Breakfast is the most important meal of the day as you grow. The meal should be wholesome and filling. A good healthy nourishing breakfast sets you up for the entire day The ideal breakfast should have lots of fibre, wholegrains, and a good balance of healthy carbohydrates, protein and essential fats.

Eating breakfast means you are more likely to get your recommended daily intake of vitamins and minerals. Breakfast positively affects your brain function and academic performance. It supports your happy brain signals produced by serotonin, helping provide a balanced state of emotional well-being. Breakfast also promotes regular meal patterns with consistent nutrient intake.

Skipping breakfast or consuming sugary foods can lead to sluggishness and irritability. Refined sugar may make you feel better temporarily, but your body soon 'crashes' from the high, leaving you exhausted or irritable. They can also deplete vital nutrients leading to fatigue and poor concentration.

If you can't face eating food first thing in the morning, try bringing it in your lunchbox. Sip on a homemade smoothie throughout the morning or have your granola later with some fruit pieces to snack on.

Sweet & Spiced Granola

Serves 8

Homemade granola is food you can depend on as it keeps in a sealed container or glass jar in a dry cupboard for up to a week once prepared. This favourite granola recipe is so scrumptious and you can have it for breakfast, a snack, in your lunchbox, or even as a dessert with the stewed apple and rhubarb. It's amazing stuff! I hope you like it and it will serve you well! Once plated, sprinkle your favourite fruit or seeds if you wish.

You'll Need:
- Oven
- Large mixing bowl
- 25cm baking tray
- Greaseproof paper
- Wooden spoon
- Small saucepan
- Oven gloves

Ingredients for Baking:
- 250g oat flakes
- 100g sunflower seeds
- 1 tbsp xylitol
- 1 tsp ground cinnamon
- ½ tsp ground turmeric
- A pinch fine salt
- 2 tbsp raw coconut oil

To be added after baking:
- 2 tbsp desiccated coconut
- 2 tbsp shelled hemp seeds

Timing
Prepping: 5 mins
Cooking: 40 mins

1. Preheat the oven to 170°C. Cover the baking tray with a sheet of greaseproof paper.

2. Add the oat flakes, sunflower seeds, xylitol, cinnamon, turmeric and salt to a large mixing bowl and stir them together with a wooden spoon until evenly mixed.

3. Melt the coconut oil in a small saucepan over a medium heat, then pour the oil carefully into the large mixing bowl and stir in with the rest of the mixed ingredients.

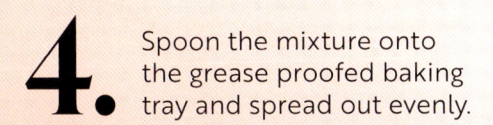

4. Spoon the mixture onto the grease proofed baking tray and spread out evenly.

5. With an oven glove, place the baking tray into the oven for 30 minutes. Every 10 minutes, use an oven glove to take the baking tray out and mix around the granola with a wooden spoon. This ensures that all of the ingredients are cooked evenly.

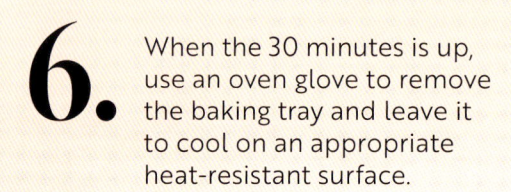

6. When the 30 minutes is up, use an oven glove to remove the baking tray and leave it to cool on an appropriate heat-resistant surface.

7. Once cooled, use a wooden spoon to mix in the desiccated coconut and hemp seeds. Transfer the granola to a container and seal. Your tasty granola will keep for 7 days in a cool, dry area.

Trivia Tidbits!

Cinnamon regulates blood sugars to help maintain energy levels.

Sunflower seeds are a good source of many nutrients which support your immune system.

The powerful spice turmeric is known as a 'healing food' when consumed within the body.

Storage

After food shopping, store your ingredients in the correct areas of the kitchen whether it be dry goods (ambient), chilled (refrigerator) or frozen (freezer). Make sure you have space in these storage sections of your kitchen when planning your shopping list.

Unopened cans, jars, and pre-packed items should be kept in dry kitchen cupboards.

Fresh fruit and vegetables are perishable foods which means they will decay if they are left out of a dry cupboard or refrigerator. Make sure that they are stored correctly to avoid food waste.

Berries should be stored in the refrigerator along with any pre-prepared fruits such as sliced pineapple.

Unripened tomatoes and avocadoes are best left out of the refrigerator, as they usually ripen well on a sunny window in the kitchen.

Root vegetables such as carrots and parsnips can be stored in the refrigerator. Potatoes and onions can be stored in a dry cupboard.

Frozen fruits should be kept in the freezer.

It's handy to be prepared with reusable food-grade resealable containers for storage, batch cooking or leftovers. You can buy these in homeware stores, food wholesalers or independent health food stores.

The first rule of storing food is to make sure that cooked food has been cooled to room temperature. You can then portion into food containers and seal with a lid. It's best practice to stick a label with the date written on it of when you prepared the food so you know what it is and how long it has been in storage.

Cooled food can then be kept in the refrigerator and used within 3 days. If you want to keep it for longer, follow the same process and place it in the drawer of the freezer for another time. Food can be frozen for up to 3 months.

When you're ready to eat the frozen portions, make sure you defrost the food completely in the refrigerator before reheating in the oven until piping hot. Ask an adult to help you until you have a routine.

Get Smart!

Rhubarb is a vegetable, and is a great source of vitamin K beneficial for bone and muscle health.

Apples are a good source of the fibre pectin which is a vital digestive enzyme to aid our digestion.

Stewed Apple & Rhubarb

Makes 500ml

You'll Need:
- Chopping board
- Small knife or dinner knife
- Teaspoon
- Bowl
- Peeler
- Small saucepan
- Measuring jug
- Wooden spoon
- Citrus Juicer
- Dish cloth

Timing
Prepping: 10 mins
Cooking: 20 mins

Ingredients:
- 2 Bramley cooking apples peeled, cored and chopped into 2cm cubes
- 1 stalk of rhubarb, topped and tailed, sliced into 2cm cubes
- 100g xylitol
- 100ml water
- 1 tsp raw coconut oil
- ½ lemon

Rhubarb is one of the first signs spring is here. A season so rich with so much growth around us from herbs to veggies to fruits. I usually stock up on local rhubarb during the springtime and freeze what I have prepared so I can use it whenever I want during the autumn or winter months to make bakes and snacks. Rhubarb is delicious when stewed with apple and is perfect with the granola recipe in this cookbook as a breakfast, snack or dessert. If you can't source rhubarb, add another apple or pear instead. This recipe will keep refrigerated for up to 3 days, or you can freeze in an appropriate container to use again. Enjoy!

1. Place the chopped apple and rhubarb into a small saucepan with the xylitol and water.

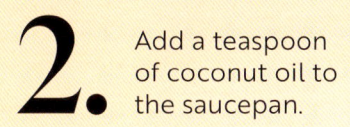

2. Add a teaspoon of coconut oil to the saucepan.

3. Stir everything together with a wooden spoon over a low heat for a minute. Juice the lemon carefully into the saucepan, stir and pop a lid on. Leave for 8 minutes, stirring occasionally. Be careful taking the lid off as it will be hot and the mixture may spit.

4. Once the fruit is stewed and soft, remove the pan from the heat and leave to cool for 10 minutes on an appropriate heat-resistant surface.

Eat as a granola topping, with yoghurt or by itself. Leftovers will keep for 3 days in the fridge.

Fun Facts!

Bread is one of the most ancient recipes known to us.

Bread is a great source of nutritious amino acids arginine and lysine beneficial for our skin health. Oats are a good source of beta-glucans which help to look after our heart health.

Oatylicious Bread

Timing
Prepping: 10 mins
Cooking: 60 mins

Makes 1 Loaf

Homemade bread is an important recipe to have because it is such a kitchen staple which can accompany so many meals. Baked bread is gorgeous with homemade soup. It's fantastic toasted with homemade dips. And it's always nice to have sliced homemade bread in the centre of the table at lunch or dinner time. This bread recipe is super quick and very wholesome. Enjoy!

You'll Need:
- Oven
- Measuring jug
- Loaf tin
- Large mixing bowl
- Wooden spoon
- Oven gloves
- Knife

Ingredients:
- Extra virgin olive oil or raw coconut oil to grease the loaf tin
- 300g oat flakes
- 400ml homemade oat cream (see recipe on page 28) or plant-based yoghurt
- 1 tbsp extra virgin olive oil
- 2 tbsp maple syrup (or syrup from brown rice, dates or oats)
- Pinch of fine salt
- 30g milled seeds
- 2 tbsp sesame seeds
- 1 tsp bicarbonate of soda
- 1 tsp baking powder

1. Preheat the oven to 180°C. Grease a 1-pound loaf tin with some olive or coconut oil.

2. In a large mixing bowl, stir in all the ingredients one by one folding them all together with a wooden spoon until you have created a sticky bread dough.

3. Transfer the dough to the loaf tin carefully with a wooden spoon, making sure you get every last bit.

4. Smooth the dough into the corners of the tin (it may only be 3/4 full but that's ok)

5. Scatter some more sesame seeds on top of the dough before placing in the oven.

6. With oven gloves pop the tin into the oven for 50 to 60 minutes, until golden-brown on top. After cooking, use oven gloves to take the tin out of the oven and leave to cool for at least 20 minutes on a heat-resistant surface.

7. Use a blunt dinner knife to separate the bread loaf from the edges.

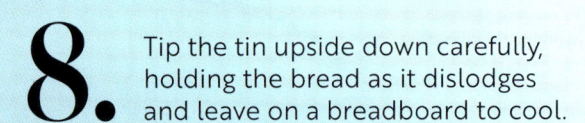

8. Tip the tin upside down carefully, holding the bread as it dislodges and leave on a breadboard to cool.

Meal Planning

Cooking from scratch means we know exactly what is in our food and allows us to choose good quality ingredients.

It is good practice to plan meals in advance where possible. It will save time, money and food waste and it will give you things to look forward to! It's nice to know that you'll be cooking and eating your favourite meal for dinner!

Top tips for meal planning:

1. Aim for a variety of meals over the course of the week.

2. Make sure you include everyone's favourite meal in the plan.

3. Use up ingredients you already have in the fridge and cupboards.

4. Make sure you use items with a short use-by date first so that nothing goes to waste.

5. If you're going to be busy one night, cook a double-portion in advance, so all you have to do is reheat the second serving!

6. Check that you have at least 5 different fruit and veg in your plan each day.

Preparing food in the kitchen is caring for yourself and others. It's looking after your body by giving it the best nutrition. It's a time for chatting together and sharing stories as we prepare a meal. It can also be a chance to celebrate occasions such as a birthday, having friends over, or even winning a sports match at school.

Remember that cooking ingredients in a different way can make them taste totally different so if you don't like it once, give it another chance!

Insider Info!

Yeast is also used in the production of kombucha for gut health, plus it is a key component of biofuels to heat homes.

Shelled hemp seeds are a good source of iron, containing around a third of the iron you require each day.

Flour was discovered around 6000 BC when wheat seeds were crushed between stones.

The Family Bread

Timing
Prepping: 130 mins
Cooking: 30 mins

Makes 1 Loaf

This bread recipe is fun to make and requires a lot of kneading which is a great upper arm workout. You'll be a superhero before you know it. This recipe is used again later as the dough for the homemade pizza. So, it's a bit of a multi-use recipe. This recipe receives a lot of positive feedback so it's a good one to make for friends and family.

You'll Need:
- Wooden spoon
- Large mixing bowl
- Measuring jug
- Clean tea towel (dampened with water)
- Oven
- Baking tray
- Oven gloves

Ingredients:
- 250g wholemeal flour
- 250g white self-raising flour
- Handful sunflower seeds
- Handful shelled hemp seeds
- 1 sachet dried yeast (7g)
- A pinch of salt
- 350ml lukewarm water

1. With a wooden spoon and a large mixing bowl, mix both of the flours, seeds, yeast and salt together well with the water to form a dough. (Add a little water if the dough is too dry or some flour if it's too wet.)

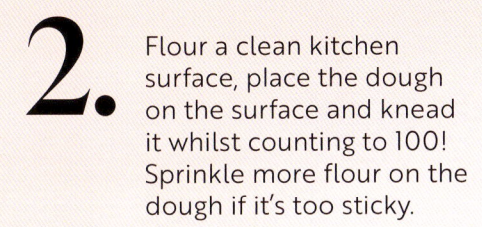

2. Flour a clean kitchen surface, place the dough on the surface and knead it whilst counting to 100! Sprinkle more flour on the dough if it's too sticky.

3. Once complete place the dough back into the mixing bowl and cover with a damp clean tea towel. Leave for a couple of hours in a warm place and you should notice the dough rising to double its original size.

4. Preheat the oven to 250°C. Dust a baking tray with flour.

5. Tip the dough out of the bowl onto a floured surface and shape it into a flat ball.

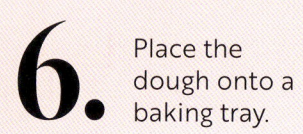

6. Place the dough onto a baking tray.

7. With an oven glove put the baking tray into the oven carefully and bake for 20 minutes then lower the heat to 220°C and bake for another 10 minutes.

8. Take the tray out of the oven carefully with an oven glove and leave the bread to cool.

Cleaning Up

It's lots of fun to prepare recipes and cook your meals, but you can't cook without making a mess! It's important to clean up after you've prepared and eaten the food, but there's no reason that can't be fun too! Put on your favourite music and have a sing and a dance whilst you put things away. Or involve a sibling and make tidying up into a competition. Perhaps see who can put away the most things in 5 minutes?

The more cooking you do, the more of a routine you will have for cleaning up. Here is my checklist for tidying the kitchen after I've finished cooking:

- Put away any opened packets or storage containers into cupboards or the refrigerator. Make sure they are sealed so they do not spoil.
- Wash any empty food storage containers for use another time.
- Clean out recyclable food packaging and put them into the correct recycling bins (or store them ready to take to the recycling centre).
- Return any unused crockery or cutlery to their designated areas in the kitchen.
- Dispose of any food waste into the appropriate bin.
- Seal leftovers into food containers and leave to cool. Refrigerate or freeze to eat another day.
- Clean food off plates and then put into the dishwasher, or wash them by hand.
- Wash any cooking pans or baking trays in warm soapy water (remember to change the water if it gets too dirty!)
- Put the dishwasher on once it is full.
- Wipe down kitchen surfaces, including the hob.
- Sweep the floor and mop if required.
- Put any dirty dishcloths and cleaning cloths into the laundry if used.

Smoothies!

Smoothies are such a great way to use up your favourite fruits from the kitchen fruit bowl. I use a plant-based milk to combine everything into a delicious drink – it's so quick and easy to do.

All these recipes will keep refrigerated until the next day in a sealed bottle or container – just remember to shake or stir before drinking. Use the method below with any of the ingredient combinations listed in the following recipes.

Makes Two
200-250ml Shakes

Timing
Prepping: 5 mins
Cooking: 10 sec

1. Add all the ingredients to a blender. Make sure the blender lid is securely on.

2. Blend for 10 seconds until all is smooth. Remove lid. Pour into a glass and serve immediately. Or pour into a sealed bottle and keep in the refrigerator for the next day. Will keep for 24 hours.

Oz Smoothie

The Oz smoothie is the first smoothie I made, inspired by my time living in Australia. The natural sweetness will help maintain your energy throughout the day.

- 1 ripe banana
- 100g of fresh stemmed strawberries
- 1 handful of blueberries
- 1 tsp of pea protein powder
- A dash of maple syrup
- 250ml of plant-based milk

Roto Loco Smoothie

The Roto Loco smoothie was christened at the local maternity hospital (called the Rotunda) in Dublin, Ireland. It was named by Cathy Hyland Ryan who works with a dedicated team to bring babies into the world. It tastes just like a tropical holiday!

- 165g of fresh pineapple, peeled, cored, chopped
- 1 ripe banana peeled
- 1 tbsp of light tahini
- ½ tsp of turmeric powder
- 1 tbsp of coconut flakes
- 1 tsp of raw coconut oil
- 250ml of plant-based milk

Eye-Opener Smoothie

This is one of my favourites to drink in the summertime with its yummy nutty flavour. It's a great way to top up your fruit and vegetable intake.

- 1 carrot peeled and sliced
- 1 ripe banana peeled
- 80g of frozen mango
- 1 tbsp of peanut butter
- 250ml of plant-based milk

Avo Nice Day Smoothie

Ripe avocado makes such a lovely base for smoothies and creates such a fab green smoothie colour, mellow and calming. I love this recipe as it is nutritious and delicate.

- 1 small avocado flesh
- 1 ripe banana
- 1 handful of baby spinach leaves
- 1 tsp of light tahini paste
- 250ml of plant-based milk

Everyday Veggie Stock

Makes 1.25 Litres

Did you know nutrient dense veggie stock is one of the oldest recipes in the world because it is used to create so many other dishes? Making your own veggie stock for soups, cooking grains and other dishes is a very sustainable homemade staple recipe. It's very simple using carrot, onion and celery plus any veggie skins you may have kept to one side during preparing vegetables. It's very handy to keep an empty container near where you are food prepping for this reason and you'll have a fridge full of stock before you know it! It is best to keep stock in batches in appropriate freezer containers for freezing, for whenever you would like to use it.

You'll Need:
- Chopping board
- Small knife or dinner knife
- Measuring jug
- Medium sized saucepan
- Wooden spoon
- Sieve
- Resealable food-grade container

Timing
Prepping: 10 mins
Cooking: 45 mins

Ingredients:
- 2 medium onions chopped
- 2 medium carrots chopped
- 2 celery sticks chopped
- Any extra fresh vegetable skins or dried herbs (thyme/rosemary) you may have left-over
- 1.25 litres of water
- Pinch fine salt
- Pinch black pepper

1. Put all the ingredients into a medium sized saucepan and cover with water. Bring to the boil, and simmer for 40 minutes, stirring occasionally with a wooden spoon. Season with salt and pepper.

2. After 40 minutes turn the heat off and leave the stock to cool. Once cooled completely strain the stock carefully with a strainer from the saucepan into a container (best to use a clean sink area in case of spillage) and store the container sealed in the refrigerator for up to 3 days. Or pour into small plastic containers and freeze for use later.

Onions are a good source of quercetin which is an anti-inflammatory healing inflammation within the body.

Carrots are a good source of vitamins beneficial for overall eye health.

Celery is a natural diuretic which can help reduce any bloating within the body.

Mind Blowing!

Hearty Veggie Soup

Noooo Way!

Extra virgin olive oil is an essential fat very beneficial for heart and skin health

Parsnips are a good source of anti-fungal properties beneficial for gut health.

Timing
Prepping: 15 mins
Cooking: 75 mins

Soup provides so much for our lives now and forever. So much veggie goodness enriches us, it's so simple and yet so powerful! It's a pleasure to share with you on your foodie journey through life! Will keep in batches refrigerated for up to 3 days once cooled. Also, will freeze in batches for whenever you require.

Makes 3 Litres

You'll Need:
- Chopping board
- Small knife
- Measuring jug
- Peeler,
- Large saucepan
- Wooden spoon
- Tongs
- Hand-held blender
- Soup ladle

Ingredients:
- 1 tbsp extra virgin olive oil
- 1 large onion peeled and finely chopped
- Half a celery stick finely chopped
- 8 carrots peeled and sliced
- 2 parsnips peeled and sliced
- 1 sweet potato peeled and chopped into cubes
- 2 courgettes sliced
- 1.25 litres of Everyday Veggie Stock (see my recipe on page 50)
- 100ml plant-based milk
- 1 bouquet garni (a small bunch of dried herbs infused in a small food grade paper bag)
- Pinch fine salt

1. Place olive oil in a large saucepan and heat over a medium heat. Add the onions and celery, fry for a few minutes stirring occasionally with a wooden spoon and reduce to a low heat.

2. Put the plant-based milk to one side and add the rest of the ingredients. Increase the heat until it is boiling then simmer for 45 minutes on a low heat, stirring occasionally with a wooden spoon. Stir in the plant-based milk and simmer for a further 15 minutes.

3. Turn off the heat and remove the bouquet garni bag from the soup with tongs.

4. Very carefully, use a hand blender to blend the soup until thick and smooth (ask an adult to do this for you if necessary). Leave to cool slightly, then use a soup ladle to serve the soup into serving bowls or a soup flask for school.

This soup is perfect to serve with a slice of your freshly baked bread (see my recipes on page 40 and 44)!

Spice Up Hummus

Makes 250g

It's the little things in life that mean the most. Homemade hummus is simple and healthy but tastes amazing. It's great to accompany falafel, veggie croquettes or veggie meatballs. Hummus is so easy to make once you have a good blender or a food processor. Once you triumph, you will be preparing hummus all the time! Try different spices to create your own recipes and flavours. This is just a stepping-stone recipe to guide you to begin with. Hummus keeps for up to 3 days in the refrigerator in a sealed container.

You'll Need:
- Blender
- Chopping board
- Small knife or dinner knife
- Strainer
- Wooden spoon
- Citrus juicer

Timing
Prepping: 10 mins
Cooking: 30 mins

Ingredients:
- 125g canned chickpeas drained
- 1½ tbsp light tahini paste
- 3 cloves garlic peeled
- 1 tsp ground cumin
- 1 tsp ground turmeric
- ½ tsp ground coriander
- ½ tsp garlic salt
- Juice from 1 lemon
- 2 to 3 tbsp plant-based milk
- 2 tbsp extra virgin olive oil

1. Add all ingredients to a food processor or blender with the lid firmly fixed (ask your adult for assistance if required).

2. Pulse for 20-30 seconds until the mixture is smooth. Remove the lid carefully.

3. Use a wooden or large dessert spoon to remove hummus from the jug carefully into a serving bowl.

Did You Know?

Chickpeas are a good source of fibre supporting heart health and your digestive system.

Tahini is made from sesame seeds which are a good source of calcium beneficial for bone health.

Fresh lemon juice is a good source of vitamin C beneficial for cold season protection.

Baba Ganoush Hummus

Makes 500ml

Timing
Prepping: 15 mins
Cooking: 40 mins

You'll Need:
- Oven
- Oven gloves
- Blender
- Chopping board
- Small knife or dinner knife
- Baking tray
- Greaseproof paper
- Strainer
- Citrus juicer

Ingredients:
- 2 aubergines with stalks removed
- 8 cloves garlic peeled
- 5 tbsp extra virgin olive oil
- 220g canned chickpeas & drained
- Juice of 2 lemons
- 1 ½ tbsp light tahini
- Pinch of salt
- 2 to 3 tbsp plant-based milk
- 1 tsp ground cumin

I just love the name Baba Ganoush, it sounds like something really appetising to prepare and eat. And it is! This yummy Lebanese roasted aubergine dip is very tasty and satisfying, especially with falafel and sandwiches, at picnics and parties. It's super yummy in a small container in your lunchbox with carrot or celery sticks. It's really nice with sweet potato burgers too. Have fun preparing this dip as it will provide great nourishment for you. Aubergines are readily available and are really delicious roasted. This dip will keep in the refrigerator for up to 3 days in a sealed container.

1. Preheat the oven to 180°C. Place a sheet of greaseproof paper onto a baking tray and fit.

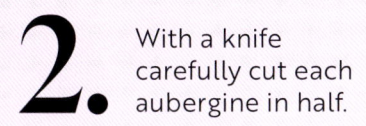

2. With a knife carefully cut each aubergine in half.

3. Then carefully slice each piece lengthways and place each strip onto the baking tray beside a clove of garlic.

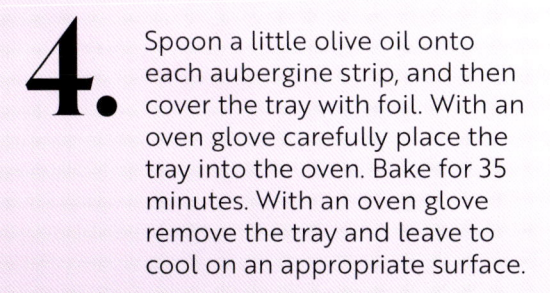

4. Spoon a little olive oil onto each aubergine strip, and then cover the tray with foil. With an oven glove carefully place the tray into the oven. Bake for 35 minutes. With an oven glove remove the tray and leave to cool on an appropriate surface.

5. Spoon the aubergine strips, garlic, chickpeas, lemon juice, tahini, salt, plant-based milk and cumin into a blender or food processor. Make sure the lid is firmly fixed (ask your adult for assistance if needed).

6. Blend for 20 seconds until all is smooth. Then pour your Baba Ganoush mixture into a bowl. Your Baba Ganoush will keep for 3 days in a refrigerator once sealed.

Fancy a dip?

Baba Ganoush is a classic dip and tastes great with all kinds of veg, which can be a great way to introduce new foods into your diet.

Try this recipe with carrot sticks, celery, cucumber or even asparagus, for a tasty treat throughout your day!

Did You Know?

Aubergines are a good source of fibre and B vitamins.

Tahini paste is a good source of tryptophan which creates happy hormones called serotonin within the body.

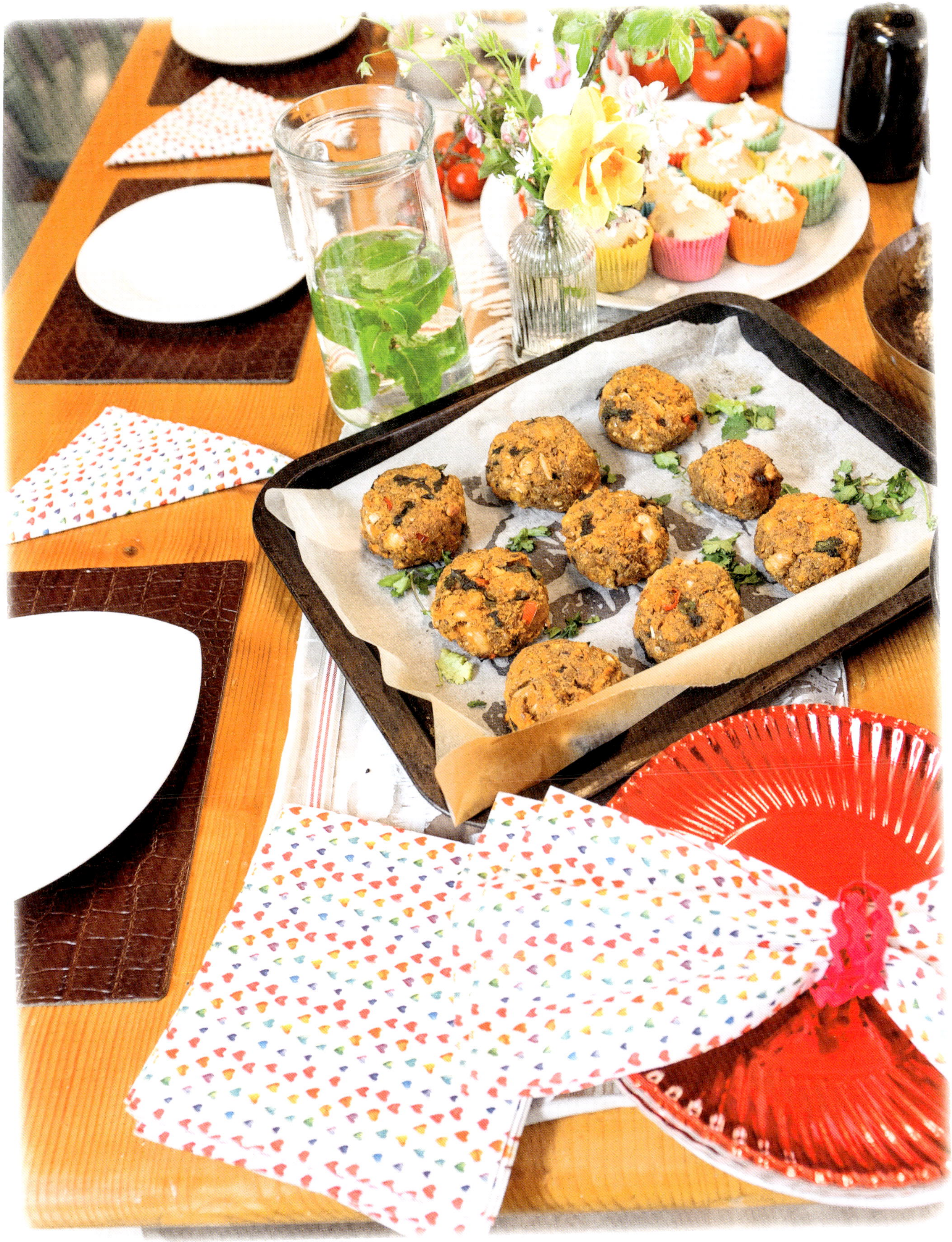

Basil Sunflower Pesto

Makes 250ml

Having a basil pesto recipe is a must for every kitchen. It can be used in a variety of ways – as a dip with falafel, a spread for sandwiches or as a sauce with pasta, rice or quinoa. I use sunflower seeds instead of pine nuts for this basil pesto recipe. They taste even nicer if toasted on a dry pan before blending, if you have the time. The homemade oat cream makes this dip super creamy (see page 28 for recipe). This pesto will keep in a sealed container in the refrigerator for up to 3 days.

You'll Need:
- Blender
  Measuring jug
- Chopping board
- Small knife or dinner knife
- Citrus juicer

Ingredients:
- Handful of fresh basil leaves
- 50g sunflower seeds (toasted makes more flavoursome pesto)
- Juice of 1 lemon
- 2 tbsp extra virgin olive oil
- 200ml oat cream (see page 28 for recipe)
- Pinch of fine salt

Timing
Prepping: 5 mins
Blend: 15 secs

1. Add everything to a blender and blitz for 15 seconds until smooth. Make sure the blender lid is securely on. Use a spoon or spatula to transfer to bowl.

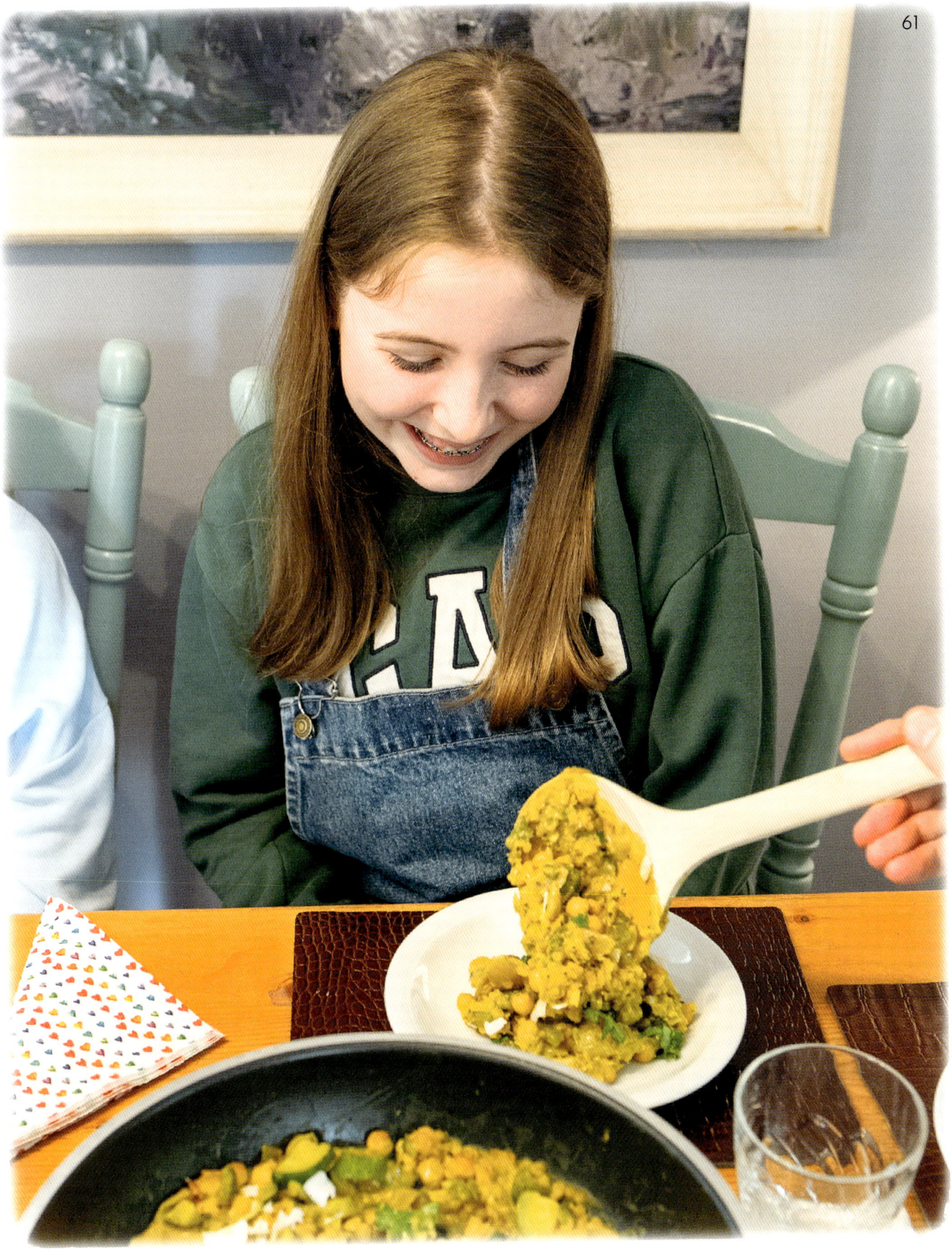

Tamari Toasted Seeds

Makes a small side dish bowl

Timing
Prepping: 2 mins
Cooking: 3 mins

Tamari Toasted Seeds are the yummiest snack which can be used for your lunchbox nibbles but also can be sprinkled on so many dishes in this cookbook to give extra texture and nourishment. They are so easy to make, once you've mastered the technique you'll aways have a tub of seeds to hand.

You'll Need:
- Frying pan
- Wooden spoon
- Small serving bowl

Ingredients:
- Two handfuls of pumpkin seeds
- Two handfuls of sunflower seeds
- 1 tbsp of tamari

1. Scatter all the seeds into a small dry frying pan with the tamari. Place the pan on a medium heat for a couple of minutes until the seeds start sizzling a little and turn golden.

2. Using a wooden spoon, remove the toasted seeds from the pan onto a small bowl. Leave to cool and then tuck in!

Sunflower seeds are a good source of minerals and work really well milled in a blender for baking.

Pumpkin seeds are a good source of Zinc, an important nutrient for our health, especially our skin health.

Tamari is a gluten-free soy sauce perfect for adding flavour to so many dishes especially stir fries.

Did You Know?

Sundried Tomato Falafel

Falafels are the perfect all-rounder for the school lunchbox providing so much goodness to take you through the rest of your day with a smile on your face. They are so fun to make and prepare. They taste great and are even yummier with hummus, pesto or dips! I like to make a pitta or wrap sandwich with fresh rocket leaves, some tomato and hummus for lunch, it's delicious! Also great for parties and picnics. They keep for up to 3 days refrigerated (if there's any left!) You can freeze it in batches to use later.

Makes about 20 Falafels

Timing
Prepping: 25 mins
Cooking: 25 mins

You'll Need:
- Food processor
- Large bowl
- Wooden spoon
- Oven
- Oven gloves
- Chopping board
- Small knife or dinner knife
- Sieve
- Baking tray

Ingredients:
- 220g canned chickpeas drained
- Pinch dried parsley
- 2 tsp cumin ground
- 1 tsp coriander ground
- 4 fresh cloves garlic peeled & chopped finely
- 1 handful of fresh coriander leaves
- 10 sundried tomatoes from a jar, drained
- 150g milled seeds
- Pinch of salt

1. Preheat the oven to 220°C. In a food processor or a large blender jug add all ingredients and place the lid on the processor or blender carefully. Pulse for 20 to 30 seconds until all the ingredients are roughly chopped (be careful not to blend into a smooth paste).

2. Transfer the mixture into a large bowl, using a spoon to make sure all the mixture is removed completely. If the mixture is too wet, stir in some more milled seeds to dry out the dough slightly before creating falafel.

3. With clean hands shape your mixture into a golf ball sized ball and repeat. If the mixture is too wet knead in more milled seeds. Place all the falafel onto the baking tray 1 inch apart in rows. Have fun creating your own falafel, round, flat, or burger bite style.

4. Using oven gloves, carefully place the baking tray in the oven on the middle or top shelf (ask an adult to assist you if required). Allow 20-25 minutes for the falafel to bake. Remove the baking tray from the oven with oven gloves and leave to cool on an appropriate surface.

So Cool!

Tomatoes are a good source of lycopene beneficial for healthy skin.

Garlic is a good source of allicin supporting our immune system and is released when chopped, blended or crushed.

Super Power Veggie Croquettes

Makes 20

Homemade veggie croquettes are yummy golden nuggets of goodness. These energy-boosting bites are perfect to have as a snack, in your lunchbox, or at picnics. Try these with pesto, hummus or Baba Ganoush as a dip, to add more scrumptiousness. The recipes for these can also be found in this cookbook.

You'll Need:
- Oven
- Oven gloves
- Chopping board
- Small knife or dinner knife
- Garlic crusher
- Baking tray
- Heat resistant surface
- Food processor
- Large mixing bowl

Ingredients:
- 8 carrots peeled and sliced
- 2 parsnips peeled and sliced
- 2 tbsp raw extra virgin coconut oil
- 1 tbsp maple syrup
- 160g sweetcorn
- 160g petit pois
- 6 roasted peppers from a jar, finely chopped
- 2 garlic cloves peeled & crushed
- 1 handful of fresh coriander leaves
- 2 tbsp harissa paste
- 1 tsp of vegan bouillon powder
- 2 pinches of fine salt
- 250g milled seeds

Timing
Prepping: 40 mins
Cooking: 100 mins

1. Preheat the oven to 180°C. Cover a baking tray with a sheet of greasproof paper. Place the sliced carrots and parsnips on a grease-proofed baking tray. Dot the coconut oil over the carrot and parsnips and mix around to evenly coat.

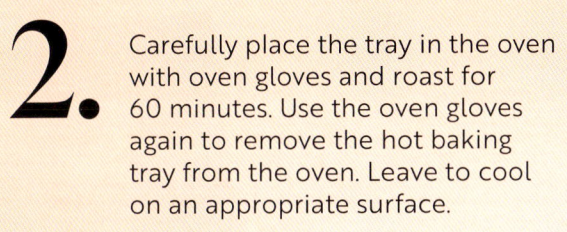

2. Carefully place the tray in the oven with oven gloves and roast for 60 minutes. Use the oven gloves again to remove the hot baking tray from the oven. Leave to cool on an appropriate surface.

3. Put the milled seeds to one side. Add the cooked carrots and parsnips into a food processor with the rest of the rest of the ingredients. Ask an adult to assist if required with locking in the lid of the processor securely.

4. Pour the blended mixture into a large mixing bowl and add the milled seeds. With clean hands mix the ingredients and knead to create a dough.

5. Mould the dough into small cylinder-shaped croquettes and place on a floured baking tray in rows. Repeat this until the baking tray is full of croquettes.

6. Place in a preheated oven using your oven glove for 40 minutes at 180°C until golden. Remove from the oven carefully with an oven glove and leave to cool on an appropriate heat-resistant surface

Did You Know?

Sweetcorn is a good source of lutein, a nutrient which supports your eye health as you get older.

Parsnips are available all year round, and are a good source of fibre and vitamin C packing a nutritional punch of goodness.

Petit pois are a type of pea that will help with healthy growth, as peas are a good source of folic acid and zinc.

My favourite lunchbox recipes include:

- Sweet and Spiced Granola
- Berry Mango Soaked Oats
- Sliced homemade Family Bread
- Hearty Veggie Soup
- Sundried Tomato Falafel
- Spice Up & Baba Ganoush Hummus
- Super Power Veggie Croquettes
- Veggie Meatballs with Tasty Sundried Tomato Sauce
- Tamari Toasted Seeds
- Apple Banana Bites
- Fluffy Flapjacks
- Lemon and Ginger Muffins
- Nana's Fruit Tea Slice

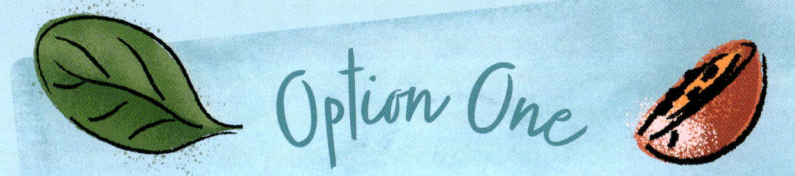

Option One

2 toasted slices of homemade bread with homemade hummus, falafel, rocket leaves and sliced tomato. One homemade Choco Apple Banana Bite on the side, and a small container of toasted seeds to snack on.

Option Two

3 veggie croquettes with a small container of Basil and Sunflower Pesto as a dip. A few cherry tomatoes on the side with an apple or banana for something sweet. Enjoy with a bottle of homemade smoothie.

Option Three

A flask of homemade soup with a slice of bread on the side. A small container of stewed fruit with a sprinkling of granola on top makes a nice sweet treat, accompanied by a satsuma and a bottle of fresh water.

Tasty Sundried Tomato Sauce

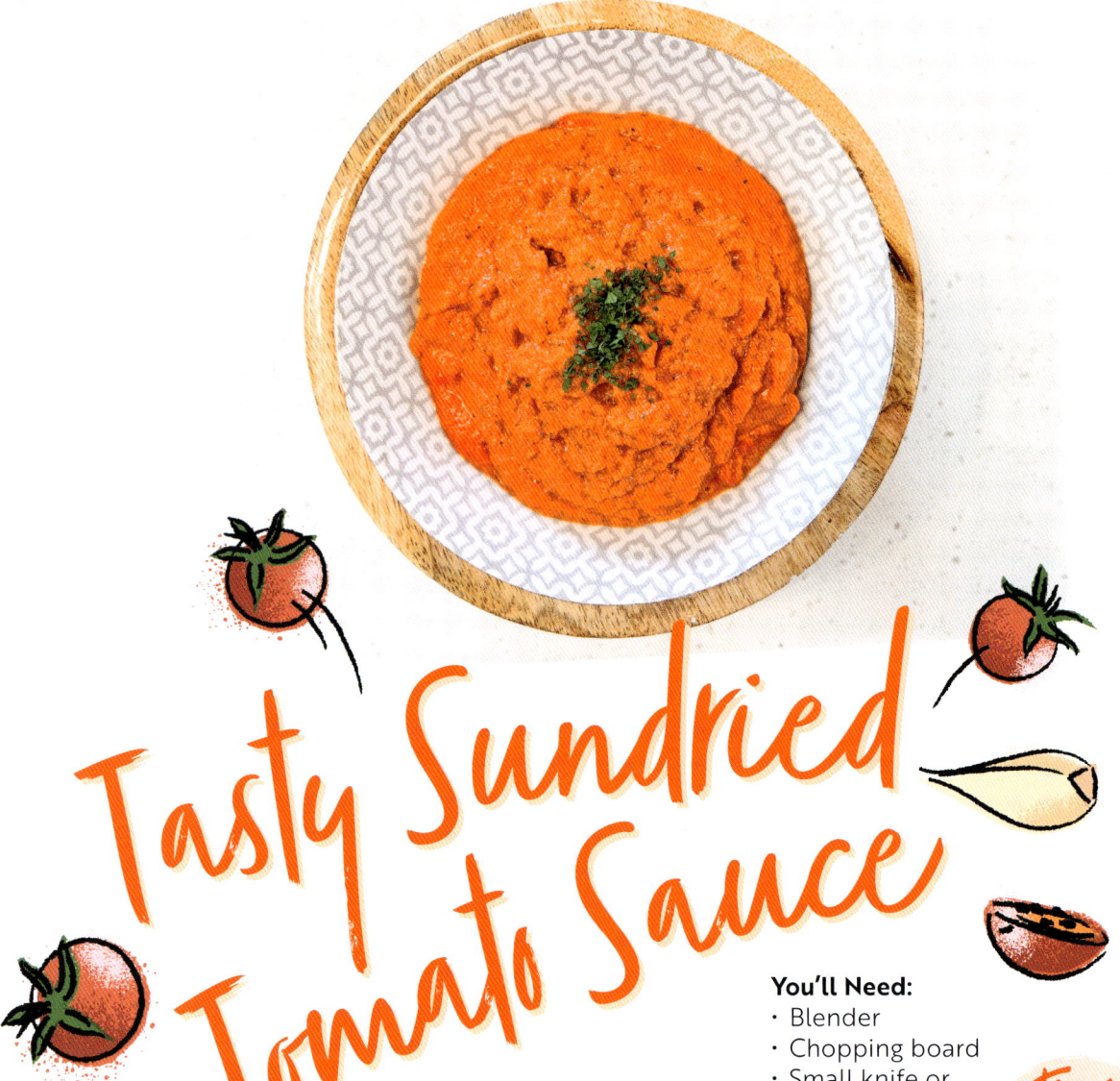

Makes 500ml

I got the opportunity to work in Rome, Italy for the summer when I was 18 years old. There was a greengrocer beside where I lived, with the most amazing fresh produce, that I visited all the time to prepare my evening meals. It reminded me of my parents' greengrocer where I grew up and it made me feel like I was at home. This is one of the recipes I would use all the time to mix with cooked pasta or rice, cous cous or quinoa. It is a very flavoursome tomato sauce and the sundried tomatoes make it even richer. I think you will like this recipe and hope you'll treasure it forever.

You'll Need:
- Blender
- Chopping board
- Small knife or dinner knife
- Resealable food-grade container
- Saucepan
- Wooden spoon

Ingredients:
- 400g can chopped tomatoes
- ½ jar (77g) sundried tomatoes drained
- 1 tsp brown rice miso paste
- 1 tsp dried oregano
- 1 tsp dried basil
- 4 garlic cloves peeled
- 1 tsp harissa paste

Timing
Prepping: 5 mins
Blend: 15 Secs

1. Add all the ingredients to a blender with the lid on tightly and blend for 15 seconds, ask an adult for assistance if necessary.

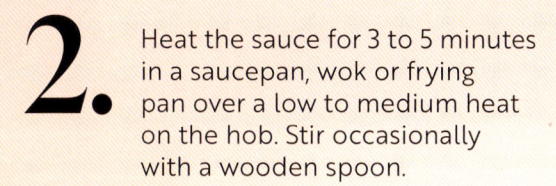

2. Heat the sauce for 3 to 5 minutes in a saucepan, wok or frying pan over a low to medium heat on the hob. Stir occasionally with a wooden spoon.

3. If you don't want to eat the sauce straightaway, avoid heating it up and pour straight from the blender into a reusable jar or container. Make sure to spoon all the sauce from the blender jug with a spatula and seal to keep it fresh in the refrigerator for up to 3 days.

Did You Know?

Tomatoes are classified as fruits as they contain seeds.

Oregano is very popular in Italian cooking creating the most delicious sauce for cooked pasta dishes.

Harissa is a Tunisian chilli paste, herbs and spices beneficial for vitamin E which is an antioxidant protecting our skin.

The magic ingredient in the veggie meatballs is millet. A tiny bead-shaped gluten-free grain which happens to be a very good source of plant protein. Each grain contains up to 20% plant protein. It is also a good source of magnesium and B vitamins. I have been working with millet for nearly 20 years and it's one of my favourite whole food grains to use not only with savoury recipes but also baking recipes. It's so nourishing and I always feel good after eating this cooked grain. It works perfectly in this recipe for meatballs along with miso, mushroom and herbs.

Veggie Meatballs

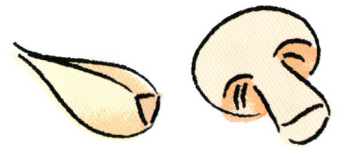

These are also handy snack bites to have for lunch boxes, but I love it with sundried tomato sauce as an evening meal (see page 70 for recipe). They keep in the refrigerator in a sealed container for up to 3 days. And will freeze in appropriate sealed containers for whenever you want.

Makes 28

You'll Need:
- Medium saucepan
- Measuring jug
- Chopping board
- Small knife or dinner knife
- Strainer
- Baking tray
- Oven
- Oven glove
- Food processor
- Large mixing bowl
- Heat resistant surface

Ingredients:
- 200g millet grain
- 500ml veg stock or water
- 250g mushrooms washed and sliced
- 220g canned butter beans drained
- 50g oat flakes
- 2 tbsp brown rice miso paste
- 100g oat bran
- 100g milled seeds
- 2 tbsp nutritional yeast
- 1 handful of fresh coriander leaves
- 1 fresh red chilli cored, seeded & finely chopped
- 2 garlic cloves peeled finely chopped
- 1 tsp dried oregano
- 1 tsp dried basil
- 4 tbsp extra virgin olive oil

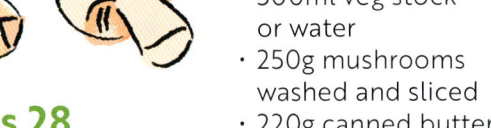

Timing
Prepping: 30 mins
Cooking: 40 mins

1. Cover the millet grain with veg stock in a medium saucepan. Heat over a high heat to bring to the boil then turn the heat down and simmer for 8 minutes, stirring occasionally.

2. Take off the heat when the millet grain plumps up and softens, and soaks up all the stock. Meanwhile, preheat the oven to 180°C and dust a baking tray with some flour.

3. Pulse the mushrooms, butter beans and oat flakes in a food processor to create a coarse mixture.

4. In a large bowl add all the remaining ingredients together one by one and mix together with the cooked millet and the mushroom mix. Combine with a wooden spoon or fork until well mixed.

5. With clean hands shape your veggie meatballs into a golf ball sized ball and repeat. Place all the veggie meatballs onto the baking tray 1 inch apart in rows.

6. With oven gloves place the baking tray in the oven carefully on the middle or top shelf, ask an adult to assist you if required. Allow 30 minutes for the veggie meatballs to bake. Remove the baking tray from the oven with oven gloves and leave the baking tray to cool on an appropriate surface.

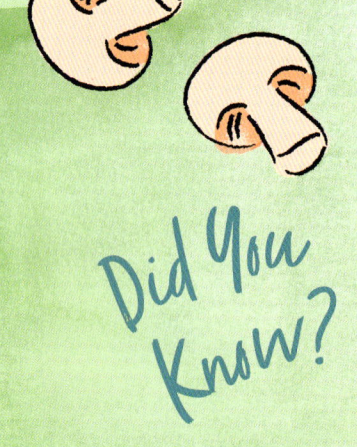

Did You Know?

Mushrooms are a good source of chromium and vitamin D. Vitamin D is produced in mushrooms as they are grown under special heat lamps similar to sunlight.

Miso paste is a good source of plant protein and makes a wonderful cup of instant soup with 1 teaspoon of the paste.

Staple Foods

Dried goods, such as pasta and rice are good store cupboard ingredients. They have a long shelf life, are inexpensive to buy, and can quickly be transformed into a satisfying meal. Give them a try with some of the recipes in this cookbook, such as cooked pasta with sundried tomato sauce or cooked rice with the lentil dahl recipe.

Pasta

Pasta is a fun food that takes minutes to cook. There are many varieties of pasta as you may know. Visit your local independent health food store and see what's on offer.

My favourite is wholewheat penne, fusilli, tagliatelle and spaghetti. I also love different grain or pulse pastas like quinoa, corn, rice and lentil.

To cook pasta simply follow the directions on the back of your individual pasta packet for the best results as every pasta can be different in cooking times. Normally I put the uncooked pasta into a pot and cover it with cold water. Bring to a boil stirring to separate the pasta so it is not sticking. Boil until pasta is al dente – when the pasta is soft and intact. Remove pasta from heat and drain carefully in a colander and run the cold tap over the pasta to rinse.

Cooked pasta can be stored in a container with cold water for up to 2 days refrigerated only.

Rice

The best rice for you nutritionally and for life is short or long-grain brown rice. Contains B vitamins, plant protein and dietary fibre. It has a chewy texture and nutty flavour. It takes longer to cook than white rice, about 40 minutes.

Rinse and simmer with a pinch of salt in 2 parts water to 1 part rice for approx. 40 minutes. Remove from heat and allow to steam for 10 minutes with the lid on.

Cooked rice can be stored in a container for up to 2 days in the refrigerator.

Chickpea Coconut Lentil Dahl

This simple and quick dinner recipe will fill your kitchen with the most exquisite scents of coconut and spices. A dahl recipe is an excellent dish to introduce you to the world of spices in a fab sharing dish for all the family. All you need is a wok and the prepped ingredients from your independent health store. If there is any left after dinner you can portion the leftovers once cooled and refrigerate for up to 3 days or freeze in suitable sealed containers for another day.

Timing
Prepping: 20 mins
Cooking: 25 mins

Serves 5

You'll Need:
- Wok
- Chopping board
- Small knife or dinner knife
- Wooden spoon
- Grater

Ingredients:
- 1 tbsp raw coconut oil
- 2 medium onions finely chopped
- 1 green pepper cored, seeded and finely chopped
- 1 courgette finely chopped
- 1 green chilli cored, seeded and finely chopped
- 1 tsp ground turmeric
- 1 tsp ground cumin
- 1 tsp ground ginger
- ½ tsp ground coriander
- 1 garlic clove peeled and finely chopped
- 1 tsp grated fresh ginger
- 1 pinch fine salt
- 220g chickpeas drained or soaked
- 200g red lentils washed
- 200ml veg stock
- 400ml coconut milk
- 1 tsp of xylitol (optional)
- 1 tbsp fresh coriander leaves

1. In a wok melt the coconut oil and add the onions, pepper and courgette. Add in the chilli, turmeric, cumin, ground ginger, ground coriander, garlic, fresh ginger, and salt and stir in well with a wooden spoon. Continue cooking over a medium heat for 5 minutes until the vegetables have softened.

2. Add the chickpeas, lentils, stock, coconut milk and xylitol. Stir to combine.

3. Leave to simmer for 15 minutes on a low to medium heat, stirring occasionally.

Serve with cooked long grain, short grain or basmati brown rice and sprinkle some fresh coriander leaves on top.

Did You Know?

Courgettes are also known as zucchini and contain 90% water content.

Lentils are a good source of fibre, plant protein and minerals.

Chickpea canned water can be whisked and used as an egg replacer in baking.

Sweet Potato Beanie Burgers

Timing
Prepping: 60 mins
Cooking: 60 mins

Makes 16

Sweet potatoes are delicious no matter how they're cooked. My sweet potato beanie burgers are always a family favourite. They are a delight to make as they bring so much colour and vibrancy into the kitchen. They are ideal for lunch or dinner and can be refrigerated for up to 3 days once cooked. Otherwise, they can be put in the freezer in appropriate containers to eat whenever you like. I love making these into proper burgers with buns, pickles and tomatoes. Plus you can add one of the delectable dips from this cookbook, such as the pesto.

You'll Need:
- Oven
- Oven glove
- Chopping board
- Small knife or dinner knife
- Peeler
- Baking tray
- Large mixing bowl
- Masher
- Strainer

Ingredients:
- 4 medium sweet potatoes, peeled and cut into medium chunks
- 150g milled seeds
- 220g butter beans, drained
- 220g chick peas, drained
- Pinch of salt
- 2 fresh garlic cloves crushed
- 1 red chilli seeded, cored, chopped finely
- Handful of fresh coriander leaves
- 2 tbsp raw coconut oil

1. Preheat the oven to 180°C. Greaseproof a 20cm baking tray. Spread out the sweet potato chunks on the tray. Distribute the coconut oil over the sweet potatoes. Pop the baking tray in the oven carefully with an oven glove and roast for 30 minutes.

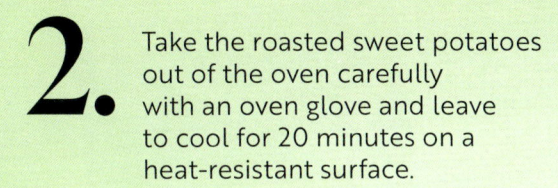

2. Take the roasted sweet potatoes out of the oven carefully with an oven glove and leave to cool for 20 minutes on a heat-resistant surface.

3. Add the cooled sweet potatoes to large mixing bowl with the garlic, chillies and coriander.

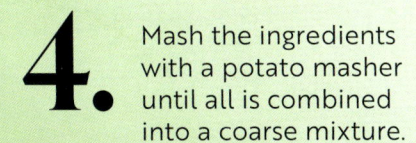

4. Mash the ingredients with a potato masher until all is combined into a coarse mixture.

5. Preheat the oven to 220°C. With a wooden spoon stir in the milled seeds, butter beans, chickpeas and salt, with the sweet potato mixture and mix together until you are left with a dough-like mixture.

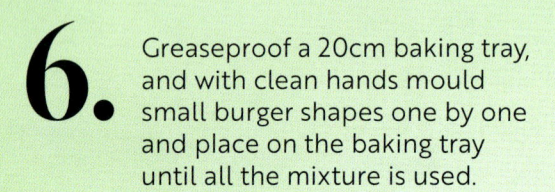

6. Greaseproof a 20cm baking tray, and with clean hands mould small burger shapes one by one and place on the baking tray until all the mixture is used.

7. Place the baking tray in the oven for 30 mins until the burgers are golden. Remove the baking tray with an oven glove and leave to cool on a heat-resistant surface.

These burgers are also gorgeous with hummus or Baba Ganoush on the side as a dip.

Did You Know?

Fresh coriander makes gorgeous pesto, use the recipe in the book and replace the basil leaves with coriander leaves.

Butter beans make delicious hummus, use the recipe in the book and replace the chickpeas with the butter beans.

81

Rockin' Ratatouille Quinoa

Timing
Prepping: 10 mins
Cooking: 25 mins

Serves 5

Quinoa is a gluten-free grain of goodness. It works perfectly with this enjoyable dish that takes minutes to prepare and cook. It's perfect for an easy dinner when you want something quick to make. This recipe also works well with pasta, rice, noodles or cous cous. This will keep in a refrigerator for up to 3 days in a sealed container. Or portion for the freezer in sealed containers to have for another time.

You'll Need:
- Medium saucepan
- Wok
- Measuring jug
- Wooden spoon
- Chopping board
- Small knife or dinner knife
- Peeler

Ingredients:
- 200g quinoa
- 500ml cold water
- 1 tsp vegan bouillon
- 1 tbsp extra virgin olive oil
- 1 red onion peeled and finely chopped
- 1 courgette peeled and finely chopped
- 1 pepper cored, seeded & chopped
- 2 roasted peppers from jar, finely chopped
- 1 handful of baby spinach leaves
- 12 cherry tomatoes halved
- 2 tbsp homemade plant-based pesto (see page 60 for recipe)
- A pinch of salt

1. Add the quinoa to a medium saucepan and cover with cold water with a teaspoon of vegan bouillon. Bring to the boil on a high heat (takes around 3 minutes) stirring occasionally. Once boiling, lower the heat to very low and put a lid on the pan. Leave for 10 minutes, stirring occasionally until all the water is absorbed and the quinoa cooked & fluffy. Set aside to cool.

2. Heat oil in a wok and add the onions, courgette and peppers, stirring with a wooden spoon until everything is soft. This takes 3 to 5 minutes.

3. Add in the spinach and tomatoes, stirring well for around 2 minutes, until the spinach has wilted.

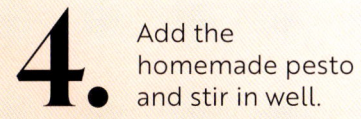

4. Add the homemade pesto and stir in well.

5. Stir in the cooked quinoa with a pinch of salt and mix with the wooden spoon. Leave to cook on a medium heat for 3 minutes until everything is hot.

6. Once everything is warm, serve in small serving bowls. Perfect for a quick family meal, or portion into small airtight containers for an easy packed lunch option. Enjoy!

Did You Know?

Red peppers are actually green peppers that have been allowed to ripen on the vine.

Spinach is an economical nutrient-dense veggie which should be used more in everyday cooking as it is so beneficial for your long-term health.

Quinoa is also a good source of fibre and B vitamins.

Teenage Kicks

As you enter your teenage years the food you eat can really support your physical and mental health.

Iron is a nutrient that is often low in teenagers. Iron deficiency can contribute to tiredness and poor cognition so make sure you get adequate amounts from foods such as lentils, chickpeas, hemp seeds, spinach and quinoa.

Other nutrients in greater demand are calcium which helps build strong bones, plus zinc for cognitive function and to make neurotransmitters, which keep your mood on an even keel.

Having adequate amounts of good-quality protein is vital for the growth and repair of tissues so make sure they include pulses, nuts and seeds.

Omega 3 fats can help keep your skin in check, along with plenty of fruit and vegetables which provide a whole spectrum of nutrients and antioxidants. Hydration helps keep the skin clear too and is also key for keeping focus and concentration and avoiding fatigue.

Nutty Veggie Noodles

Timing
Prepping: 15 mins
Cooking: 15 mins

Serves 5

If you're a fan of peanut butter, veggies and noodles, you'll love this quick flavoursome wok recipe. This recipe is fabulous for a quick lunch or dinner. It also works as a crowd-pleaser if your friends are round for dinner. If there is some left it will keep in a sealed container in the refrigerator for up to 3 days.

You'll Need:
- Blender,
- Wok
- Measuring jug,
- Wooden spoon
- Chopping board
- Small knife or dinner knife
- Citrus juicer

Ingredients:

Sauce
- 2 tbsp peanut butter
- Juice of 1 lime
- 2 tbsp tamari
- 2 tbsp sweet chilli sauce
- 1 pinch vegan bouillon
- 80ml oat cream (see page 28 for recipe)
- 50ml plant-based milk

Stir Fry
- 4 wholewheat noodle nests
- 1 tbsp raw coconut oil
- 1 onion peeled and finely chopped
- 1 courgette finely chopped
- 1 green pepper cored, seeded, and finely chopped
- 1 broccoli cut into florets
- 4 handfuls baby spinach leaves

1. Add all the sauce ingredients to a blender with lid securely on. Blend for 15 seconds.

2. Pour or use a spoon/spatula to transfer the sauce to a small bowl and set aside.

3. In a wok add the nests and cover with hot water, simmer on a medium heat for 5 mins until nests separate & soften. Use a wooden spoon to help pull the nests apart. Drain water carefully (ask an adult to assist if required).

4. Set the cooked noodles to one side in a bowl.

5. Add the oil to the wok over a medium high heat until sizzling slightly and carefully stir all the veggies into the wok.

6. Keep stirring occasionally for 5 mins or until the veggies soften.

7. Add the peanut sauce and return the noodles to the wok. Mix everything together and continue to stir occasionally for a further 2 to 3 minutes until everything is well combined and hot through.

Did You Know?

Spinach is one of the richest sources of lutein for optimal eye health and vitamin K for bone health.

If you leave limes in the sunlight and roll them before using them you will have more juice from the lime when squeezed.

Broccoli is one of the most nutrient dense foods, especially antioxidant vitamin C.

Eating Together

Mealtimes vary with the ebb and flow of the year. From September to June, lunch will often be on the go and straight from your lunch box. But at weekends and during holiday times try to take the time to prepare food together and eat together with a proper sit-down meal involving your family and friends.

Come together, away from work, relax, chat and swap stories whilst preparing yummy, tasty food.

During the summer or weekends, meals can stretch between a late lunch and early dinner – this is completely ok!

For this purpose, I felt it was important to share with you a handful of easy plant-based lunch and dinner recipes for you to prepare and share with family and friends.

I developed these recipes to be as quick and easy as possible. It means they are great to make during the school week, but feel free to use them on weekends and during holiday times too. Mealtimes are a great time to bond, tell stories and discuss what is on your mind. Involve everyone in the preparation, eating the meal and - of course - the tidying and washing up!

When you're eating, discuss the food: the taste, texture, the smell, the presentation. What could be added next time? What ingredient would you swap? How does the food make you feel? As well as enjoying mealtimes you may also find there are other benefits like better digestion and stress relief.

Your friends and family will praise and appreciate all your effort in creating such happiness, which will bring great confidence for you on your onward journey with cooking as a life skill.

Did You Know?

You can sprinkle some nutritional yeast on your meal as a nice alternative to parmesan cheese.

Spinach is a good source of calcium and magnesium beneficial for bone health.

Vegtastic Pizza

One of the best memories you'll have throughout life is making a homemade pizza to share with your family, there's nothing like it! The sense of fulfilment is immense. We may be used to seeing pizzas being made in awe at our local pizzeria. Now you're bringing the pizzeria home to your kitchen with this delicious recipe in 2 parts, the pizza dough, and then the toppings. Once you're used to the routine of pizza making you will be making your own homemade pizzas all the time. Have fun creating your own pizza toppings, this is only the starting point for you to fly!

Makes 12 Slices

You'll Need:
- Wooden spoon
- Large mixing bowl
- Clean tea towel
- Chopping board
- Small knife or dinner knife
- Measuring jug
- Baking tray
- Rolling pin
- Frying pan
- Wooden spoon,
- Heat resistant surface

Timing
Prepping: 140 mins
Cooking: 20 mins

Ingredients:

Pizza Dough
- 250g wholemeal flour
- 250g white self-raising flour
- A handful of sunflower seeds
- A handful of shelled hemp seeds
- 1 sachet of dried yeast (7g)
- A pinch of salt
- 350ml warm water

Pizza Topping
- 1 tbsp extra virgin olive oil
- 1 tsp tamari
- 250g sliced mushrooms
- 1 clove of fresh garlic finely chopped
- 1 handful of fresh coriander leaves
- 3 handfuls of baby spinach leaves
- 150g vegan cheese slices or cheese of your choice
- 1 tbsp nutritional yeast
- 1 tsp garlic salt

1. With a wooden spoon and a large mixing bowl, mix both of the flours, seeds, yeast and salt together well with the water to form a dough. (Add a little water if the dough is too dry or some flour if it's too wet.)

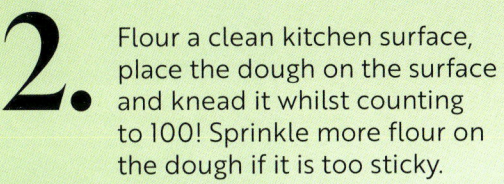

2. Flour a clean kitchen surface, place the dough on the surface and knead it whilst counting to 100! Sprinkle more flour on the dough if it is too sticky.

3. Once complete place the dough back into the mixing bowl and cover with a damp clean tea towel. Leave for a couple of hours in a warm place.

4. Once the dough has doubled in size, tip it out carefully onto a floured clean surface. With a rolling pin, roll the pizza dough into a rectangular shape to fit a baking tray. Make sure all corners and sides are fitted with the dough into the tray. Preheat your oven to the highest temperature.

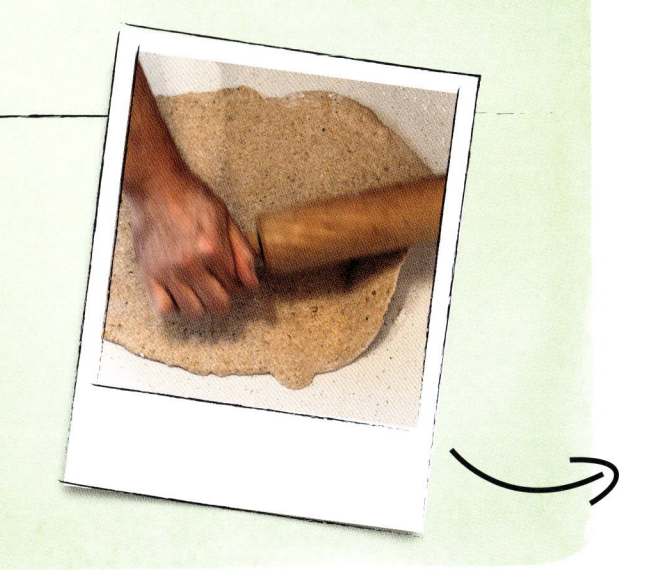

5. Brush the surface of the dough with a tablespoon of olive oil and put to one side.

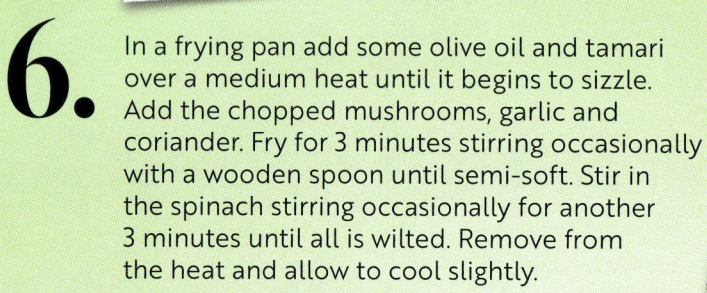

6. In a frying pan add some olive oil and tamari over a medium heat until it begins to sizzle. Add the chopped mushrooms, garlic and coriander. Fry for 3 minutes stirring occasionally with a wooden spoon until semi-soft. Stir in the spinach stirring occasionally for another 3 minutes until all is wilted. Remove from the heat and allow to cool slightly.

7. Place the sliced vegan cheese onto the dough wherever you like so all areas of the dough will be covered when the cheese is melted. Scatter the mushroom mix onto the dough. Cover all areas with the mixture with the wooden spoon. Also, sprinkle a pinch of salt and nutritional yeast over the dough. Pat down all the toppings with the wooden spoon.

8. Place the tray in the pre-heated oven carefully with an oven glove for 10 to 12 minutes. Reduce oven temperature to 190°C for last 3 minutes. Remove the tray with an oven glove and leave to cool slightly on an appropriate surface. Slice with a pizza slicer or knife (ask an adult to assist you if necessary) so you have 12 slices.

Parties and Picnics

There are lots of party and picnic recipes in this cookbook for you to prepare beforehand, the morning of or the day before the event. You can also invite your friends on the day to share in preparing the fun party recipes together with the permission and guidance of an adult to supervise.

My favourite recipes for parties and picnics in this book are: Oatylicious Bread, Sundried Tomato Falafel, Baba Ganoush Hummus, Super Power Veggie Croquettes, Basil Sunflower Pesto, Vegtastic Pizza, Tamari Toasted Seeds, Lemon & Ginger Muffins, Choco Apple Banana Bites and the Fluffy Flapjacks. 3 to 4 of these recipes will give you plenty of choice and variety at any picnic or party.

Always check the weather on the morning of your picnic. If it's a hot day make sure to bring plenty of bottled water to keep hydrated. Count how many are coming to your party or picnic and prepare the food for that number so you're not left with too much food leftover.

And HAVE FUN with the whole wonderful experience!

Party Time!

Mama's Mashed Potatoes

Did You Know?

Potatoes are a good source of fibre, with about 3g of fibre per potato working wonders for your overall health.

There are over 100 edible varieties of potato in the world.

Timing
Prepping: 10 mins
Cooking: 30 mins

Makes 700g

One of the first recipes that I was taught to make by my Mum was mashed potatoes. It is such a nourishing comfort food and easy to prepare and make! It is a versatile food recipe as it can be dished up for lunch or dinner to accompany many different meals. We use the mashed potatoes here as the topping for our veggie cottage pie.

You'll Need:
- Large saucepan
- Chopping board
- Small knife or dinner knife
- Strainer
- Masher

Ingredients:
- 8 peeled and halved potatoes (floury potatoes such as Maris Piper/Pinks/King Edward/Queens)
- 2 tbsp plant-based milk
- 1 tbsp extra virgin olive oil
- Pinch of fine salt
- Pinch of black pepper

1. Place the peeled potatoes in a large saucepan and cover with cold water. Bring to the boil over a high heat. Once the water is boiling reduce the heat to low and simmer for 20 minutes until potatoes are soft. TIP: check with a dinner knife - if you can easily cut through the potatoes then they're done!

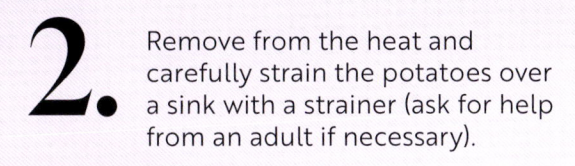

2. Remove from the heat and carefully strain the potatoes over a sink with a strainer (ask for help from an adult if necessary).

3. Return the strained potatoes back to the saucepan and add the plant-based milk, oil, salt and pepper.

4. Whilst the potatoes are still hot, mash them with a potato masher until smooth. Leave to cool slightly if you're using them for the cottage pie or serve immediately as a side for dinner time.

Wren Cottage Veggie Pie

Serves 6 to 8

This pie is a celebration meal, one for a special occasion or a Sunday sit down with the family to savour, chat over and enjoy. The recipe is named after a special place close to my heart which changed my world. It has hosted many a magical occasion which is why I named this yummy dish after one of my favourite places. It takes a little longer to prepare than some of the other recipes in the cookbook but that's the fun of it. It's all about the layering, make this recipe with love and you will cherish it forever. If you don't finish all of it, it will keep in the refrigerator for up to 3 days covered. Or you can freeze pieces in appropriate containers to have for another time.

You'll Need:
- Oven
- Oven glove
- Chopping board
- Small knife or dinner knife
- Baking tray
- Wok
- Wooden spoon
- Measuring jug
- Baking dish
- Heat resistant surface

Timing
Prepping: 40 mins
Cooking: 80 mins

Ingredients:
- 3 small aubergines
- 6 garlic cloves, peeled
- 1 tbsp extra virgin olive oil
- 300g of homemade mashed potatoes (see page 94 for recipe)
- 3 medium white onions peeled & finely chopped
- 3 carrots peeled and sliced
- 1 small sweet potato peeled and cubed
- 2 handfuls of baby spinach leaves
- 1 tbsp harissa paste
- 200g red lentils washed
- 1 tbsp vegan bouillon
- 750ml veg stock
- 1 tsp herbs de Provence

1. Preheat the oven to 180°C. Place a sheet of greaseproof paper onto a baking tray. Cut each aubergine in half, then carefully slice lengthwise with a dinner knife to create large thin slices. Place the slices onto the baking tray in heaped rows until the baking tray is full. Drizzle a little olive oil onto each aubergine slice and place the garlic cloves around the tray. Using an oven glove, place in the oven and bake for 35 minutes.

2. Take the tray out of the oven with an oven glove and leave the tray to cool on an appropriate surface.

3. Once cooled, put the roasted garlic cloves on a small plate and mash the cloves together with a fork. Then stir in the garlic into the 300g of mashed potatoes.

4. Heat olive oil in a wok over a medium heat. Add the onions and stir for a few minutes with a wooden spoon until they are golden and softened. Stir in the carrots, sweet potato, and spinach. Then add the harissa, lentils, bouillon, herbs and stock to cover the veggies. Turn the heat down to low for 10 minutes and cover with a lid. Stir occasionally until the veggies and lentils have all softened. Then set it aside and leave to cool.

5. In the meantime, add some olive oil to a large 25cm baking dish, spreading the oil out evenly across the surface. Cover the base of the dish with half of the cooked aubergine slices, then carefully spoon all the veggie mixture from the wok on top.

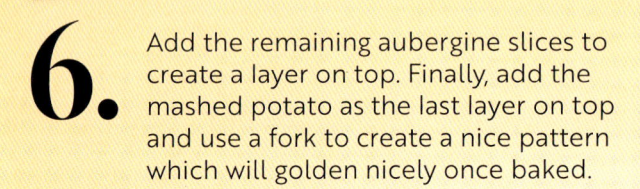

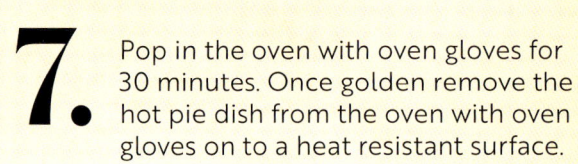

6. Add the remaining aubergine slices to create a layer on top. Finally, add the mashed potato as the last layer on top and use a fork to create a nice pattern which will golden nicely once baked.

7. Pop in the oven with oven gloves for 30 minutes. Once golden remove the hot pie dish from the oven with oven gloves on to a heat resistant surface.

Did You Know?

Aubergines are also known as eggplants as they look like a large pear-shaped egg. Aubergine contains antioxidants which repair cell damage throughout the body.

Vegan bouillon also makes a lovely quick cup of soup, just add warm water to a teaspoon of the bouillon powder.

Red lentils have one of the highest sources of plant protein in the vegetable universe.

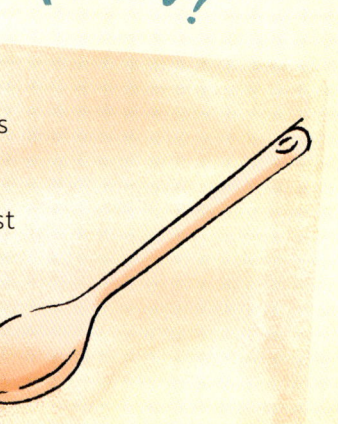

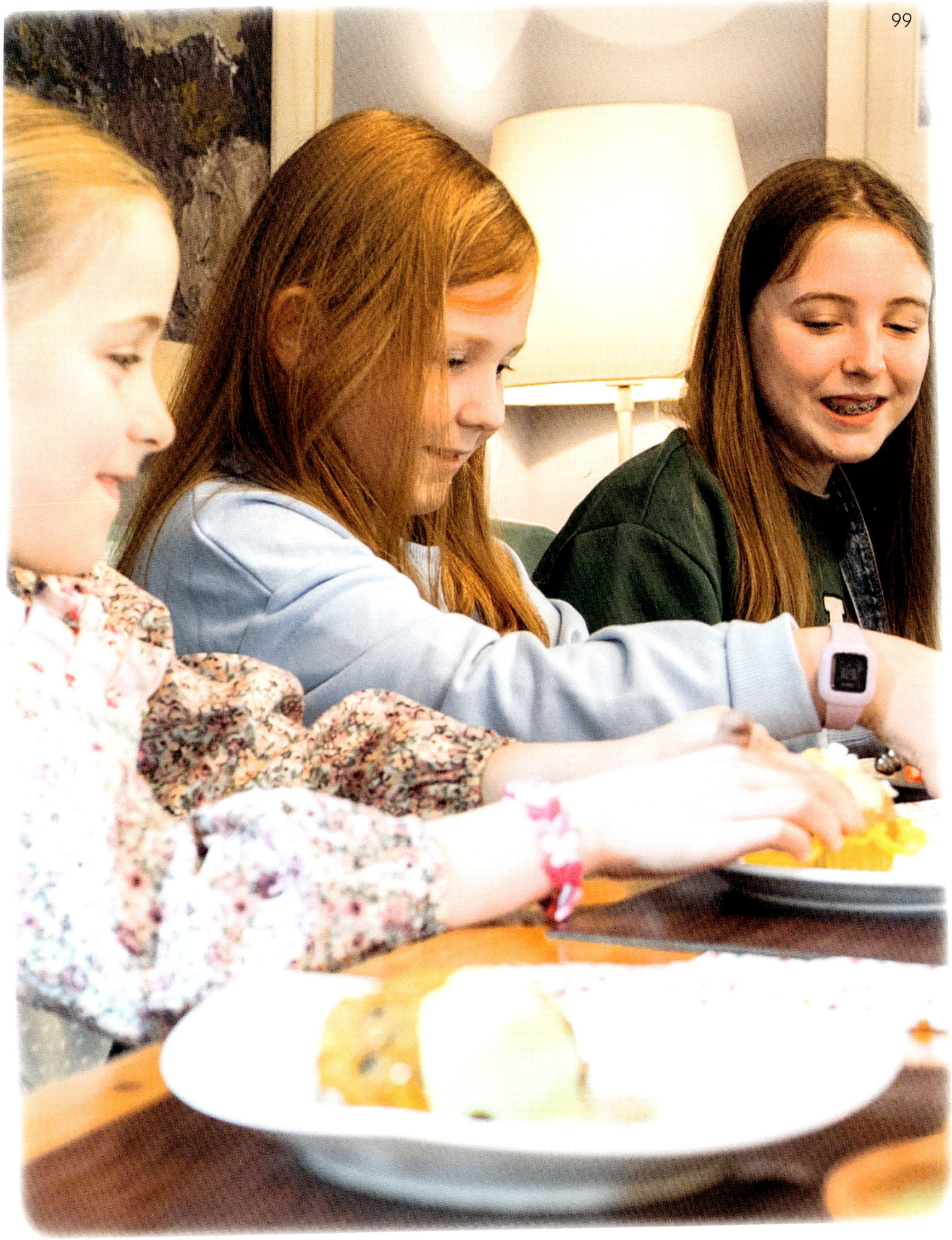

Did You Know?

Rocket is a good source of many vitamins and minerals such as calcium, magnesium and zinc.

Pear is a good source of fibre, vitamin C and E and with around 4 grams of fibre per pear

Rocket and Pear Salad

Timing
Prepping: 5 mins

This is a very easy salad recipe. Fresh rocket leaves are readily available all year round and have a lovely peppery taste. Fresh delicious pear goes so well with rocket, it's like an explosion of flavour. Good olive oil and toasted seeds make this salad a dish to accompany any meal. I first came across this combination when I lived in Sydney, Australia over 25 years ago, and it has remained with me and has stood the test of time. I feel nostalgic sharing it with you!

Makes 1 Medium Bowl

You'll Need:
- Grater
- Large salad bowl
- 2 wooden spoons

Ingredients:
- 3 handfuls of fresh rocket leaves
- 1 pear
- Pinch of salt
- A drizzle of extra virgin olive oil
- A sprinkling of toasted seeds

1. Place rocket leaves in a large salad bowl. Carefully grate the pear over the rocket leaves. Grate all around the pear until you are left with the core which you can discard.

2. Sprinkle a little salt over the salad and drizzle a little olive oil over the salad leaves.

3. With two wooden spoons toss the salad gently.

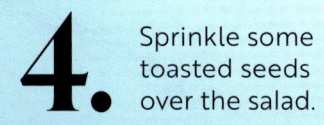

4. Sprinkle some toasted seeds over the salad.

Creamy Lasagne

Timing
Prepping: 5 mins
Cooking: 20 mins

Serves 8

You'll Need:
- Wok
- Chopping board
- Small knife or dinner knife
- Wooden spoon
- Measuring jug
- Baking dishes
- Oven
- Oven glove
- Kettle

Ingredients:
- 300g red lentils washed rinsed & drained
- 300ml of veggie stock or water
- 1 head of prepared broccoli florets
- 3 handfuls of baby spinach leaves
- 1 tbsp of vegan bouillon powder
- 3 tbsp of nutritional yeast
- 600ml of homemade oat cream (see page 28 for recipe)
- 2 tbsp of fresh coriander leaves
- 1 tbsp of fresh chilli chopped finely
- 1 tbsp of fresh garlic cloves chopped finely
- 1 tsp of smoked paprika
- ½ tsp of dried chilli flakes
- 8 sheets of lasagna
- 1 tbsp of extra virgin olive oil
- 200ml of homemade sundried tomato sauce (see page 70 for recipe)

Lasagne is a firm favourite recipe in my family. It's very comforting Italian sharing dish and the multiple layers make it fun to assemble. Take your time and once you conquer it, you will be making this buonissimo dish again and again.

1. Cover the lentils with stock or water in a wok. Bring to the boil, then simmer over a low to medium heat. Add in the broccoli florets and spinach and stir occasionally for 5 minutes.

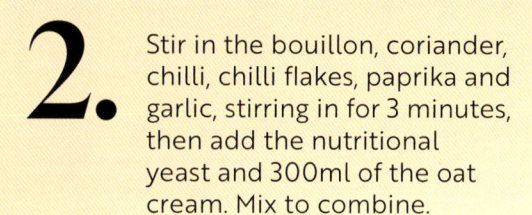

2. Stir in the bouillon, coriander, chilli, chilli flakes, paprika and garlic, stirring in for 3 minutes, then add the nutritional yeast and 300ml of the oat cream. Mix to combine.

3. Add 100ml of homemade sundried tomato sauce. Stir in for a minute. Take off the heat to cool. Preheat the oven to 180C.

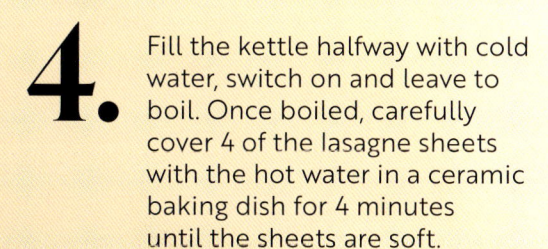

4. Fill the kettle halfway with cold water, switch on and leave to boil. Once boiled, carefully cover 4 of the lasagne sheets with the hot water in a ceramic baking dish for 4 minutes until the sheets are soft.

5. Grease the base of a separate baking dish with olive oil. Place the 4 soft sheets of lasagne on the base of the baking dish. And add 4 more dry sheets to the hot water, repeat the same method until they soften.

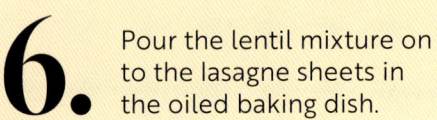

6. Pour the lentil mixture on to the lasagne sheets in the oiled baking dish.

7. Place the soft lasagne sheets on top as final layer with a sprinkling of nutritional yeast.

8. Pour on the remaining sundried tomato sauce and the remaining oat cream, mixing well with a spoon. With an oven glove place the baking dish in the oven and leave for 30 minutes until all is baked beautifully.

105

Lemon and Ginger Muffins

Makes 12 Muffins

Lemon and ginger work so well together, especially when baking moist scrumptious muffins. This recipe is easy and fun to make, particularly so with all your friends for a party. You can be really creative with the decoration. Use some raw coconut oil to grease the muffin cases to prevent the muffins sticking to the paper. You can use raisins or finely chopped dried figs instead of sultanas if you wish. The cashew lemon icing to accompany this muffin recipe is delicious.

To decorate, see cashew icing recipe on the next page.

You'll Need:
- Oven
- Oven glove
- Muffin baking tray
- Grater or zester
- Citrus juicer
- Muffin cases

Timing
Prepping: 25 mins
Cooking: 35 mins

Ingredients:
- 100ml extra virgin olive oil
- 150g xylitol
- 4 tbsp maple syrup
- 350ml homemade oat cream (see recipe on page 28) the equivalent of 3 medium eggs
- Zest and juice of 1 large lemon
- 300g self-raising flour
- 1 tsp baking powder
- 100g milled mixed seeds
- 1 tsp ground cinnamon
- 30g chopped crystalised ginger
- 30g sultanas
- 1 tbsp grated fresh ginger

107

1. Preheat the oven to 180°C. Prepare a muffin baking tray with 12 muffin cases.

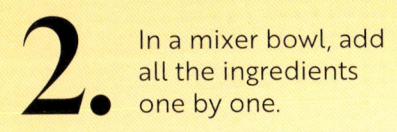

2. In a mixer bowl, add all the ingredients one by one.

3. Using an electric mixer on a medium speed, carefully mix for 2 minutes until everything is combined. (Alternatively, use a large mixing bowl and wooden spoon to mix all the ingredients.)

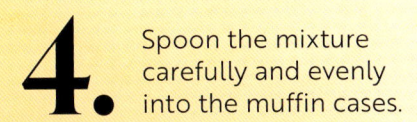

4. Spoon the mixture carefully and evenly into the muffin cases.

5. Use an oven glove to put the tray into the oven and bake for 35 minutes.

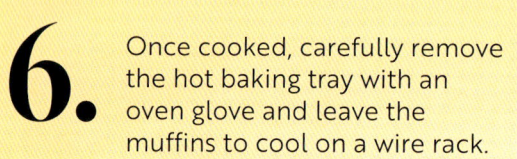

6. Once cooked, carefully remove the hot baking tray with an oven glove and leave the muffins to cool on a wire rack.

7. Once cooled decorate the muffins with cashew icing carefully with a teaspoon and grate some lemon zest on top as a finishing touch, decorate as you like.

Did You Know?

Oat bran is found within the outer layer of the oat grain and is nutrient dense with many health benefits.

Coconut oil is an excellent healthy oil for high-temperature cooking.

Ginger has many health benefits including supporting your immune system during cold and flu season.

109

Cashew Lemon Icing

Timing
Prepping: 70 mins

You'll Need:
- Blender
- Chopping board
- Citrus juicer
- Small knife or dinner knife
- Grater or zester
- Resealable food-grade container

Ingredients:
- 200g cashew nuts
- 200g coconut yoghurt
- 1 tsp vanilla essence
- Zest and juice of 1 lemon
- 2 tbsp maple syrup
- 1 tbsp raw coconut oil
- 1 pinch fine salt
- 1½ tbsp coconut flakes

1. Cover the cashew nuts in warm water in a bowl and leave to soak for an hour. Once the nuts are soaked and soft, drain the water. Add the nuts with the rest of the ingredients to a blender. Make sure the blender lid is securely on. Blend for 10 seconds until all is smooth.

2. Pour into a side dish to decorate muffins or cakes immediately. Or pour into a sealed bottle or container and keep in the refrigerator for up to 3 days.

111

Choco Apple Banana Bites

Timing
Prepping: 45 mins
Cooking: 50 mins

Makes 16 Bites

You'll Need:
- Medium saucepan
- Chopping board
- Small knife or dinner knife
- Wooden spoon
- Citrus juicer
- Measuring jug
- Baking tray
- Oven
- Oven glove,
- Small saucepan

Ingredients:
- 250g millet grain
- 600ml of water
- 3 cooking apples cored, peeled, chopped
- 2 bananas peeled and chopped
- ½ lemon juiced
- 1 tbsp maple syrup
- 150g xylitol
- 100g ground almonds
- 200g milled seeds
- 2 tsps of raw coconut oil
- A pinch of Himalayan fine salt
- 120g dark chocolate chips
- 2 tbsp of desiccated coconut

Get ready for Choco Apple Banana Bites to keep you moving throughout the day. These are absolutely delicious and perfect for a breakfast snack or lunchbox treat. They are terrific for weekends to bring with you for walks, hikes and bike rides. You can have them with or without the dark chocolate, depending on what you prefer.

1. Cover the millet grain with 600ml of water in a medium saucepan. Heat over a high heat to bring to the boil, then turn the heat down and simmer for 8 to 10 minutes, stirring occasionally with a wooden spoon until the grains plump up, soften and soak up all the water. Then remove from the heat.

2. In the meantime, grease a 36cm baking tray with some coconut oil. Preheat the oven to 180°C.

3. In the same pan as the millet, add all the remaining ingredients. Set aside the chocolate chips and desiccated coconut.

4. Stir until you have a cake dough. It's a bit of a workout but it is worth it.

5. Spoon the dough onto the baking tray and smooth out with a wooden spoon into the edges of tray.

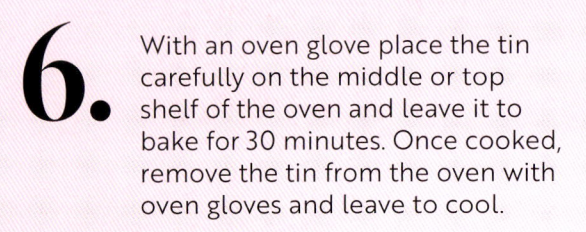

6. With an oven glove place the tin carefully on the middle or top shelf of the oven and leave it to bake for 30 minutes. Once cooked, remove the tin from the oven with oven gloves and leave to cool.

7. Whilst the traybake is cooling, melt the dark chocolate chips in a small saucepan with 1 tsp of coconut oil over a low heat.

8. Once all is melted use a dessert spoon to spread the chocolate over the bake entirely, take your time to cover all areas. Then sprinkle some desiccated coconut on top to decorate. Leave to cool.

Once cooled, pop into refrigerator for 30 mins until the chocolate has set. Then use a knife to carefully cut the bake into 16 bites.

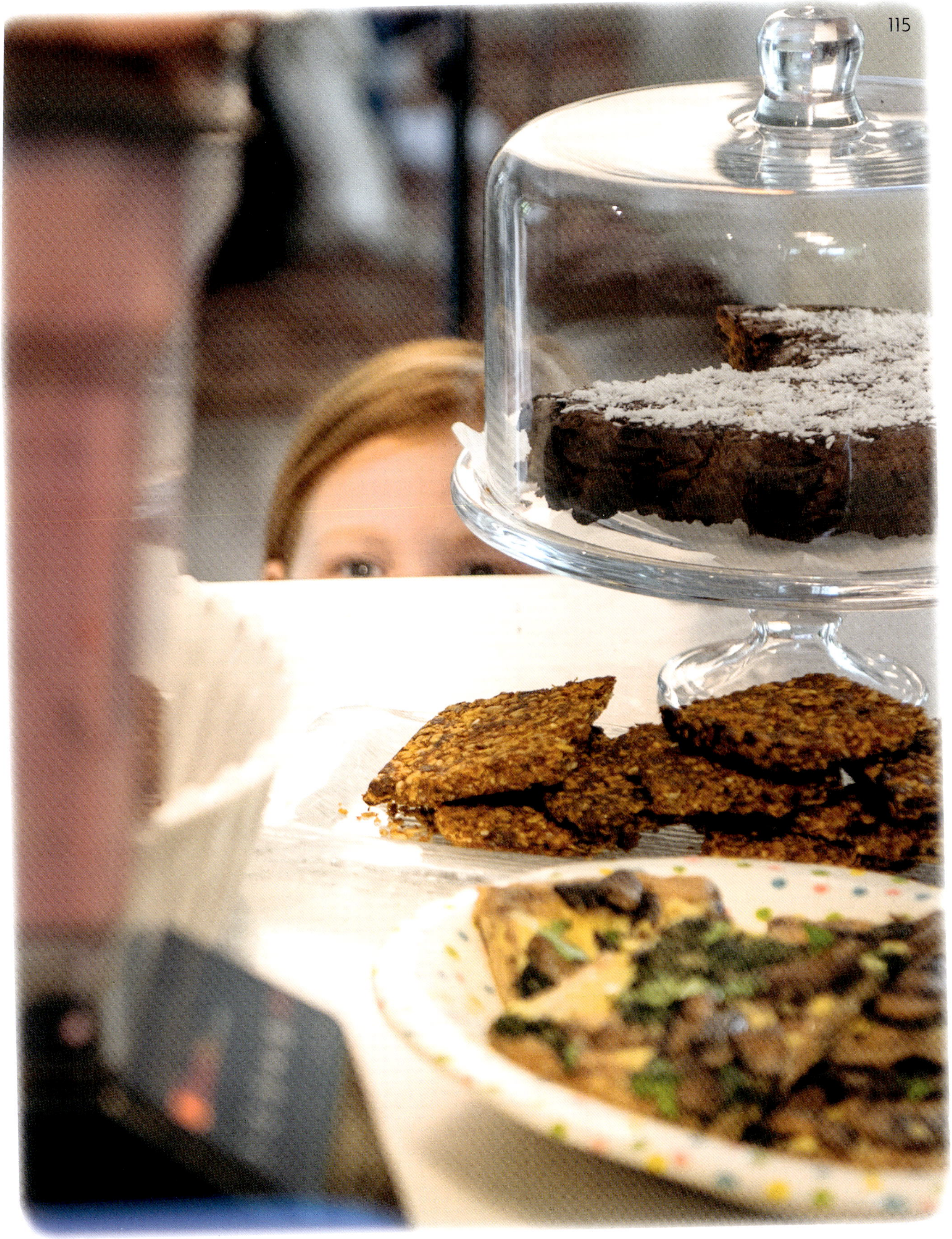

Did You Know?

Dates are a good source of protective nutrients and antioxidants which generate healthy cells within the body.

Seeds are a good source of minerals and vital nutrients for the body's organs.

Fluffy Flapjacks

Flapjacks are perfect for picnics and parties and are always a crowd-pleasing treat. My secret ingredient in these flapjacks is the sweet water the dates are soaked in. It is this water that makes them so fluffy and moreish! The oats make them rich in fibre and help you feel fuller for longer.

Timing
Prepping: 30 mins
Cooking: 30 mins

Makes 12

You'll Need:
- Oven
- Oven glove
- Baking tray
- Small saucepan
- Large mixing bowl
- Citrus juicer

Ingredients:
- 150g pitted dates
- 50ml extra virgin olive oil
- 50g raw coconut oil
- 150g xylitol
- 1 tbsp maple syrup
- 100g peanut or seed butter
- 150g oat flakes
- 50g sunflower seeds
- 1 tbsp sesame seeds
- 50g milled seeds
- 1 tsp ground cinnamon
- 1/2 tsp ground turmeric
- A pinch fine salt
- ½ orange cut into 2 quarters

1. Cover the dates with 1 cup of hot water in a small bowl. Leave for 10 minutes to cool. Take the dates out of the water one by one to chop into small pieces on a chopping board. Leave to one side. Make sure that you keep the date water.

2. Preheat the oven to 180°C. Line the base of a 23cm baking tray with baking parchment paper.

3. In a small saucepan set over a low heat, mix together the olive oil, coconut oil, xylitol, maple syrup, peanut butter and chopped dates. Stir constantly for around 8 minutes until the mixture is smooth and thick. Add the date water kept from the soaked dates to dilute the mixture.

4. In a large mixing bowl, mix the oats, sesame seeds, milled seeds, cinnamon, turmeric and salt together. Also, squeeze the juice from one of your orange quarters into the mix. Make sure no pips fall in!

5. Carefully pour the liquid ingredients from the saucepan into the mixing bowl with dry ingredients and stir well to combine.

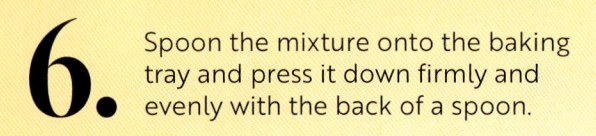

6. Spoon the mixture onto the baking tray and press it down firmly and evenly with the back of a spoon.

7. Squeeze the other orange quarter over the top of the mixture and allow it to soak in.

8. With an oven glove pop the tray carefully into the preheated oven. Bake for 20 minutes, until golden on top. Remove from the oven carefully with an oven glove.

Leave to cool and once cooled cut the bake with a knife into 4 rows widthways and 3 rows lengthways to create 12 squares. Eat straight away or store in an airtight container in the fridge for up to 3 days.

Sports Activities

Everyday exercise is so important for your health, whether it's walking, running, cycling, swimming, or playground games. Exercise will make you happier, it provides focus and promotes better sleep. If you can go outside for 1 hour each day and play with your friends and family that will be sufficient. You can break the hour up over various time periods during your day.

The best foods to boost your store of energy for physical activity are rich in complex carbohydrates: these include foods such as whole grains, fruits and vegetables.

When it comes to sports, it's important to time your meals so you use the fuel generated from your meals efficiently.

Eating two hours before any major sports activity allows time to digest and fuel up optimally.

Don't forget that refuelling after an activity is equally important, ideally within thirty minutes.

Balancing meals with carbohydrates, adequate protein and colourful foods (fruits and veggies) will provide high-octane fuel for sports activities.

Keep quick snacks on hand to provide immediate energy between meals and while on the go.

Simple snacks like apple slices with tahini paste provide both carbs and protein.

Likewise, crackers with veggie dips, toasted seed mix, homemade snack bars and bottled homemade smoothies can all be super boosters between meals.

Energy Boost!

Nana's Fruit Tea Slice

Timing
Prepping: 25 mins
Cooking: 95 mins

This fruit cake recipe is a very sentimental recipe which reminds me of my grandparents. It's a delight to prepare for a special occasion to share with friends and family. It's very easy to put together and it's so delicious with a cup of tea or coffee but especially nice with a mug of hot chocolate.

Serves 12-14

You'll Need:
- Medium saucepan
- Large mixing bowl
- Measuring jug
- Round springform cake tin
- Oven
- Oven glove

Ingredients:
- ½ tsp ground cinnamon
- ½ tsp ground turmeric
- 100g raw coconut oil
- 100ml extra virgin olive oil
- 250g xylitol
- 300g sultanas
- 125g dried cranberries
- 200ml black tea brewed
- 100ml plant-based milk
- 1 tsp bicarbonate of soda
- 1 tsp baking powder
- 300g strong white flour
- 100g milled seeds
- 1 tbsp maple syrup

1. Preheat the oven to 180°C

2. In a medium saucepan mix together the cinnamon, turmeric, coconut oil, olive oil and xylitol. Heat the mixture over a low heat stirring until everything has melted, this takes about 3 minutes.

3. Add the sultanas and cranberries. Mix in the tea, plant-based milk, bicarbonate of soda and baking powder. Stir well for a couple of minutes until all is blended. Turn off the heat.

4. In a large mixing bowl add the flour, milled seeds and maple syrup then add the mixture from the saucepan carefully and fold in with a wooden spoon.

5. Line an 8" inch round springform cake tin with greaseproof paper.

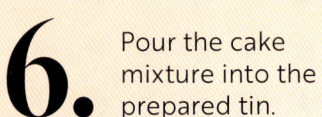

6. Pour the cake mixture into the prepared tin.

7. Place the cake tin into the oven on the top shelf carefully with an oven glove. Bake for 30 minutes on 180°C then turn down the oven temperature to 150°C and bake for a further 60 minutes. Take the cake tin out carefully with an oven glove. Leave to cool on a heat-resistant surface. Once cooled open the spring on the side of the cake tin to release the bottom of the cake tin to remove the cake efficiently on to a cake stand. Cut slices with a knife.

Did You Know?

Most black tea comes from Sri Lanka, Indonesia and East Africa and is known to be beneficial to improve focus.

Sultanas are a good source of polyphenols which are a good source of anti-inflammatory properties which aid ailments such as arthritis.

Milled seeds are a good source of zinc and you know if you're deficient in zinc by having more than 5 white spots on your fingernails.

Cacao Hot Chocolate

Makes 2 Cups

Timing
Prepping: 5 mins
Cooking: 5 mins

You'll Need:
- Medium saucepan
- Large mixing bowl
- Measuring jug
- Round springform cake tin
- Oven
- Oven glove
- Whisk

Ingredients:
- 1 ¼ tbsp cacao powder
- 1 tsp raw coconut oil
- 1 tsp maple syrup
- 1 tsp xylitol
- 250ml plant-based milk
- Pinch of Himalayan fine salt

This hot chocolate recipe is divine with Nana's fruit cake or any of the natural sweet treats in this cookbook. Ready to serve in your favourite cup or mug.

1. Heat all ingredients together in a small saucepan stirring consistently with a whisk over low to medium heat. Keep stirring for 3 to 5 minutes until you have a smooth texture with no bits. Pour into 2 cups for serving. Gorgeous with Nana's tea slice.

Nutritional Information

These tables show the amount of each nutrient in 100g, along with the reference intake (RI). This shows how much of your daily recommended intake is contained within the recipe. These figures are based on using the ingredients I have recommended. I have flagged the allergens in each recipe, but please check all your individual ingredients **very carefully** if you are cooking for someone with an allergy. The recipes are listed in A-Z order.

AVO NICE DAY SMOOTHIE

	Per 100g	%RI
Energy (Kj)	432Kj	5%
Energy (kcal)	104kcal	5%
Fat	6.5g	9%
of which saturates	1.3g	7%
Carbohydrates	9.2g	4%
of which saturates	7.1g	8%
Fibre	1.8g	7%
Protein	1.1g	2%
Salt	0.04g	1%

Allergens: Sesame

BABA GANOUSH HUMMUS

	Per 100g	%RI
Energy (Kj)	287 kJ	3%
Energy (kcal)	69 kcal	3%
Fat	2.9g	4%
of which saturates	0.4g	2%
Carbohydrates	5.7g	2%
of which saturates	1.5g	2%
Fibre	2.6g	10%
Protein	3.4g	7%
Salt	0.07g	1%

Allergens: Sesame, Soya

BERRY MANGO SOAKED OATS

	Per 100g	%RI
Energy (Kj)	287 kJ	3%
Energy (kcal)	69 kcal	3%
Fat	2.9g	4%
of which saturates	0.4g	2%
Carbohydrates	5.7g	2%
of which saturates	1.5g	2%
Fibre	2.6g	10%
Protein	3.4g	7%
Salt	0.07g	1%

Allergens: Oats

BASIL SUNFLOWER PESTO

	Per 100g	%RI
Energy (Kj)	1060 kJ	13%
Energy (kcal)	256 kcal	13%
Fat	23g	33%
of which saturates	3.4g	17%
Carbohydrates	6.5g	3%
of which saturates	2.7g	3%
Fibre	1.6g	6%
Protein	4.2g	8%
Salt	0.22g	4%

Allergens: Oats

CACAO HOT CHOCOLATE

	Per 100g	%RI
Energy (Kj)	399 kJ	5%
Energy (kcal)	96 kcal	5%
Fat	5.2g	7%
of which saturates	3.7g	19%
Carbohydrates	9.3g	4%
of which saturates	4.5g	5%
Fibre	3.1g	12%
Protein	2.1g	4%
Salt	0.08g	1%

Allergens: Oats

CASHEW LEMON ICING

	Per 100g	%RI
Energy (Kj)	399 kJ	5%
Energy (kcal)	96 kcal	5%
Fat	5.2g	7%
of which saturates	3.7g	19%
Carbohydrates	9.3g	4%
of which saturates	4.5g	5%
Fibre	3.1g	12%
Protein	2.1g	4%
Salt	0.08g	1%

Allergens: Cashews
May contain: Sesame, Soya, Sulphites

CHICKPEA COCONUT LENTIL DAHL

	Per 100g	%RI
Energy (Kj)	371kJ	4%
Energy (kcal)	89kcal	4%
Fat	5g	7%
of which saturates	4.1g	21%
Carbohydrates	7.5g	3%
of which saturates	2.2g	2%
Fibre	2.2g	9%
Protein	2.7g	5%
Salt	0.12g	2%

Allergens: Celery

CHOCO APPLE BANANA BITES

	Per 100g	%RI
Energy (Kj)	981kJ	12%
Energy (kcal)	236kcal	12%
Fat	13g	19%
of which saturates	3.1g	16%
Carbohydrates	25g	10%
of which saturates	11g	12%
Fibre	4g	16%
Protein	5.9g	12%
Salt	0.04g	1%

Allergens: Almonds, Soya
May contain: Sesame, Sulphites

CREAMY LASAGNE

	Per 100g	%RI
Energy (Kj)	721kJ	9%
Energy (kcal)	171kcal	9%
Fat	4.4g	6%
of which saturates	0.6g	3%
Carbohydrates	29g	11%
of which saturates	3.8g	4%
Fibre	1.6g	6%
Protein	3.5g	7%
Salt	0.3g	5%

Allergens: Oats, Wheat, Celery
May contain: Tree nuts

EASY-BREEZY PANCAKES

	Per 100g	%RI
Energy (Kj)	721kJ	9%
Energy (kcal)	171kcal	9%
Fat	4.4g	6%
of which saturates	0.6g	3%
Carbohydrates	29g	11%
of which saturates	3.8g	4%
Fibre	1.6g	6%
Protein	3.5g	7%
Salt	0.3g	5%

Allergens: Oats, Wheat

EVERYDAY VEGGIE STOCK

	Per 100g	%RI
Energy (Kj)	53kJ	1%
Energy (kcal)	13kcal	1%
Fat	0g	0%
of which saturates	0g	0%
Carbohydrates	2.4g	1%
of which saturates	1.9g	2%
Fibre	0.8g	3%
Protein	0g	0%
Salt	0.01g	0%

Allergens: Celery

EYE-OPENER SMOOTHIE

	Per 100g	%RI
Energy (Kj)	325Kj	4%
Energy (kcal)	77kcal	4%
Fat	2.5g	4%
of which saturates	0.5g	3%
Carbohydrates	11g	4%
of which saturates	8.8g	10%
Fibre	1.9g	8%
Protein	2.1g	4%
Salt	0.07g	1%

Allergens: Oats, Peanuts

THE FAMILY BREAD

	Per 100g	%RI
Energy (Kj)	905Kj	11%
Energy (kcal)	214kcal	11%
Fat	2.3g	3%
of which saturates	0.3g	2%
Carbohydrates	39g	15%
of which saturates	0.6g	1%
Fibre	4.2g	17%
Protein	7.4g	15%
Salt	0.3g	5%

Allergens: Wheat

FLUFFY FLAPJACKS

	Per 100g	%RI
Energy (Kj)	1747Kj	21%
Energy (kcal)	420kcal	21%
Fat	24g	34%
of which saturates	8g	40%
Carbohydrates	46g	18%
of which saturates	14g	16%
Fibre	4.1g	16%
Protein	8.9g	18%
Salt	0.06g	1%

Allergens: Oats, Peanuts, Sesame
May contain: Soya

GOOD MORNING PORRIDGE

	Per 100g	%RI
Energy (Kj)	444Kj	5%
Energy (kcal)	106kcal	5%
Fat	6.1g	9%
of which saturates	4.1g	21%
Carbohydrates	10g	4%
of which saturates	1.9g	2%
Fibre	1.4g	6%
Protein	1.9g	4%
Salt	0.04g	1%

Allergens: Oats, Sesame
May contain: Sulphites

HEARTY VEGGIE SOUP

	Per 100g	%RI
Energy (Kj)	162Kj	2%
Energy (kcal)	39kcal	2%
Fat	0.7g	1%
of which saturates	0.1g	1%
Carbohydrates	6.4g	2%
of which saturates	4.2g	5%
Fibre	2.1g	8%
Protein	0.7g	1%
Salt	0.27g	5%

Allergens: Oats, Celery

HOMEMADE OAT CREAM

	Per 100g	%RI
Energy (Kj)	451Kj	5%
Energy (kcal)	107kcal	5%
Fat	3.5g	5%
of which saturates	0.6g	3%
Carbohydrates	15g	6%
of which saturates	1.5g	2%
Fibre	1.9g	8%
Protein	2.7g	5%
Salt	0.27g	5%

Allergens: Oats
May contain: Wheat

LEMON GINGER MUFFINS

	Per 100g	%RI
Energy (Kj)	1104Kj	13%
Energy (kcal)	263kcal	13%
Fat	9.1g	13%
of which saturates	1.2g	6%
Carbohydrates	44g	17%
of which saturates	9.1g	10%
Fibre	3g	12%
Protein	5.2g	10%
Salt	0.38g	6%

Allergens: Oats, Wheat
May contain: Sesame, Soya

MAMA'S MASHED POTATOES

	Per 100g	%RI
Energy (Kj)	373Kj	4%
Energy (kcal)	88kcal	4%
Fat	1.1g	2%
of which saturates	0.2g	1%
Carbohydrates	17g	7%
of which saturates	0.9g	1%
Fibre	1.6g	6%
Protein	1.7g	3%
Salt	0.04g	1%

Allergens: Oats

NANA'S FRUIT TEA SLICE

	Per 100g	%RI
Energy (Kj)	1262Kj	15%
Energy (kcal)	302kcal	15%
Fat	13g	19%
of which saturates	4.3g	22%
Carbohydrates	48g	18%
of which saturates	18g	20%
Fibre	2.3g	9%
Protein	4.4g	9%
Salt	0.29g	5%

Allergens: Oats, Wheat, Sulphites
May contain: Sesame, Soya

NUTTY VEGGIE NOODLES

	Per 100g	%RI
Energy (Kj)	602Kj	7%
Energy (kcal)	143kcal	7%
Fat	4.4g	6%
of which saturates	1.1g	6%
Carbohydrates	19g	7%
of which saturates	4.8g	5%
Fibre	3.2g	13%
Protein	5.8g	12%
Salt	0.59g	10%

Allergens: Oats, Wheat, Peanuts, Soya
May contain: Tree Nuts, Sesame

OATYLICIOUS BREAD

	Per 100g	%RI
Energy (Kj)	1016Kj	12%
Energy (kcal)	242kcal	12%
Fat	9g	13%
of which saturates	4.8g	24%
Carbohydrates	33g	13%
of which saturates	3.2g	4%
Fibre	4.3g	17%
Protein	5.6g	11%
Salt	0.63g	11%

Allergens: Oats, Sesame
May contain: Wheat, Soya

OZ SMOOTHIE

	Per 100g	%RI
Energy (Kj)	281Kj	3%
Energy (kcal)	66kcal	3%
Fat	0.9g	1%
of which saturates	0.1g	1%
Carbohydrates	12g	5%
of which saturates	9.9g	11%
Fibre	1.6g	6%
Protein	1.4g	3%
Salt	0.04g	1%

Allergens: None known

ROCKET AND PEAR SALAD

	Per 100g	%RI
Energy (Kj)	482Kj	6%
Energy (kcal)	116kcal	6%
Fat	7.7g	11%
of which saturates	1.3g	7%
Carbohydrates	8.6g	3%
of which saturates	7.1g	8%
Fibre	2.4g	10%
Protein	2.1g	4%
Salt	0.22g	4%

Allergens: None known

ROCKIN' RATATOUILLE QUINOA

	Per 100g	%RI
Energy (Kj)	326Kj	4%
Energy (kcal)	78kcal	4%
Fat	3.4g	5%
of which saturates	0.5g	3%
Carbohydrates	7.9g	3%
of which saturates	3.3g	4%
Fibre	1.8g	7%
Protein	2.8g	6%
Salt	0.28g	5%

Allergens: Celery

ROTO LOCO SMOOTHIE

	Per 100g	%RI
Energy (Kj)	407Kj	5%
Energy (kcal)	98kcal	5%
Fat	6.2g	9%
of which saturates	3.3g	17%
Carbohydrates	7g	3%
of which saturates	6.3g	7%
Fibre	1.7g	7%
Protein	2.4g	5%
Salt	0g	0%

Allergens: Sesame, Soya
May contain: Sulphites

SPICE UP HUMMUS

	Per 100g	%RI
Energy (Kj)	626Kj	7%
Energy (kcal)	150kcal	8%
Fat	8.3g	12%
of which saturates	1.1g	6%
Carbohydrates	9.4g	4%
of which saturates	1g	1%
Fibre	3.7g	15%
Protein	7g	14%
Salt	0.32g	5%

Allergens: Sesame, Soya

STEWED APPLE AND RHUBARB

	Per 481g serving	%RI
Energy (Kj)	2019Kj	24%
Energy (kcal)	483kcal	24%
Fat	9.8g	14%
of which saturates	7.9g	40%
Carbohydrates	135g	52%
of which saturates	27g	30%
Fibre	6.2g	25%
Protein	1.4g	3%
Salt	0.02g	0%

Allergens: None known

SUNDRIED TOMATO FALAFEL

	Per 100g	%RI
Energy (Kj)	1224Kj	15%
Energy (kcal)	294kcal	15%
Fat	18g	26%
of which saturates	2.2g	11%
Carbohydrates	14g	5%
of which saturates	5.8g	6%
Fibre	9.5g	38%
Protein	12g	24%
Salt	0.14g	2%

Allergens: Sulphites
May contain: Sesame, Soya

SUPER POWER VEGGIE CROQUETTES

	Per 100g	%RI
Energy (Kj)	537Kj	6%
Energy (kcal)	129kcal	6%
Fat	7.4g	11%
of which saturates	1g	5%
Carbohydrates	8.7g	3%
of which saturates	6.6g	7%
Fibre	5.5g	22%
Protein	4.1g	8%
Salt	0.18g	3%

Allergens: Celery
May contain: Sesame, Soya

SWEET AND SPICED GRANOLA

	Per 76g	%RI
Energy (Kj)	1468Kj	17%
Energy (kcal)	351kcal	17%
Fat	17g	24%
of which saturates	3.6g	18%
Carbohydrates	36g	14%
of which saturates	0.8g	1%
Fibre	6.1g	24%
Protein	12g	24%
Salt	0.1g	2%

Allergens: Oats
May contain: Sulphites

SWEET POTATO BEANIE BURGERS

	Per 100g	%RI
Energy (Kj)	695Kj	8%
Energy (kcal)	166kcal	8%
Fat	6.4g	9%
of which saturates	0.9g	5%
Carbohydrates	19g	7%
of which saturates	8.2g	9%
Fibre	5g	20%
Protein	5.7g	11%
Salt	0.11g	2%

Allergens: Sesame Soya

TAMARI TOASTED SEEDS

	Per 100g	%RI
Energy (Kj)	2168Kj	26%
Energy (kcal)	523kcal	26%
Fat	41g	59%
of which saturates	6g	30%
Carbohydrates	15g	6%
of which saturates	1.2g	1%
Fibre	5g	20%
Protein	21g	42%
Salt	1.7g	28%

Allergens: Soya
May contain: Tree nuts, Peanuts, Sesame

TASTY SUNDRIED TOMATO SAUCE

	Per 100g	%RI
Energy (Kj)	346Kj	4%
Energy (kcal)	82kcal	4%
Fat	1.1g	2%
of which saturates	0.1g	1%
Carbohydrates	11g	4%
of which saturates	10g	11%
Fibre	2.9g	12%
Protein	2.5g	5%
Salt	0.62g	10%

Allergens: Soya, Sulphites

VEGGIE MEATBALLS

	Per 100g	%RI
Energy (Kj)	504Kj	6%
Energy (kcal)	120kcal	6%
Fat	4.6g	7%
of which saturates	0.7g	4%
Carbohydrates	12g	5%
of which saturates	1.5g	2%
Fibre	3.9g	16%
Protein	6.1g	12%
Salt	0.89g	15%

Allergens: Oats, Celery, Soya
May contain: Sesame

VEGTASTIC PIZZA

	Per 100g	%RI
Energy (Kj)	755Kj	9%
Energy (kcal)	179kcal	9%
Fat	4.2g	6%
of which saturates	2.7g	14%
Carbohydrates	28g	11%
of which saturates	0.6g	1%
Fibre	3g	12%
Protein	6g	12%
Salt	0.52g	9%

Allergens: Wheat, Soya,
May contain: Tree nuts, Peanuts, Sesame

WREN COTTAGE VEGGIE PIE

		%RI
Energy (Kj)	243Kj	3%
Energy (kcal)	58kcal	3%
Fat	0.7g	1%
of which saturates	0.2g	1%
Carbohydrates	9.5g	4%
of which saturates	3.2g	4%
Fibre	2g	8%
Protein	2.4g	5%
Salt	0.31g	5%

Allergens: Celery

About the Author

I have worked in the independent health and wellness sector for over 20 years as a wholefood chef, nutritional therapist and cookbook author!

I grew up in a corner greengrocer shop that my parents owned. They also ran the fuel merchants next door. So, it was an interesting mix of fuel and food. Hence the title of my bestselling first cookbook 'The Fuel Food Cookbook' which is dedicated to my parents and the shop. The cookbook was a first with regards to 'allergen friendly' easy recipes which were recipe favourites at our independent health food store and café in Dublin.

I learnt so much by watching my Mum cook in the kitchen. My earliest memories are of helping her peel root vegetables like potatoes, carrots and parsnips for dinner. It didn't feel like a chore, I enjoyed doing it when I finished my homework in the kitchen. The heart of the home! My Mum always taught us the basics of cooking from an early age so we had the tools and the knowledge of how to provide for ourselves no matter what.

We were lucky to be living above a greengrocer so I could select the vegetables, fruit and other essentials with my brothers and sisters to make meals together in the kitchen. Our kitchen was tiny, it was more like a pantry with everything nestled together cosily in a small space. My Mum taught us how to peel, stir, and cut with a small blunt knife and we always cleaned up afterwards, washing dirty utensils and crockery in the kitchen sink, returning items to the fridge, and keeping vegetable peels to make stock.

My upbringing made me keenly aware of the importance of eating good quality food products and understanding where the things we eat come from. I am a huge advocate of shopping local and eating organic and I am a proud ambassador for the Health Stores Ireland association. They do great work supporting independent health food shops in the community. I love sharing my passion and knowledge through my own company – Hubble Health – by giving talks and cooking demonstrations in schools, colleges, and workplaces, and of course, by writing recipe books like this one!

I hope you've enjoyed this book and have been able to find your favourite new recipes. It's all about having fun in the kitchen, eating well, and sharing food with your friends and family. Enjoy putting your own twist on the recipes, show off your new skills, and you'll be an expert chef in no time!

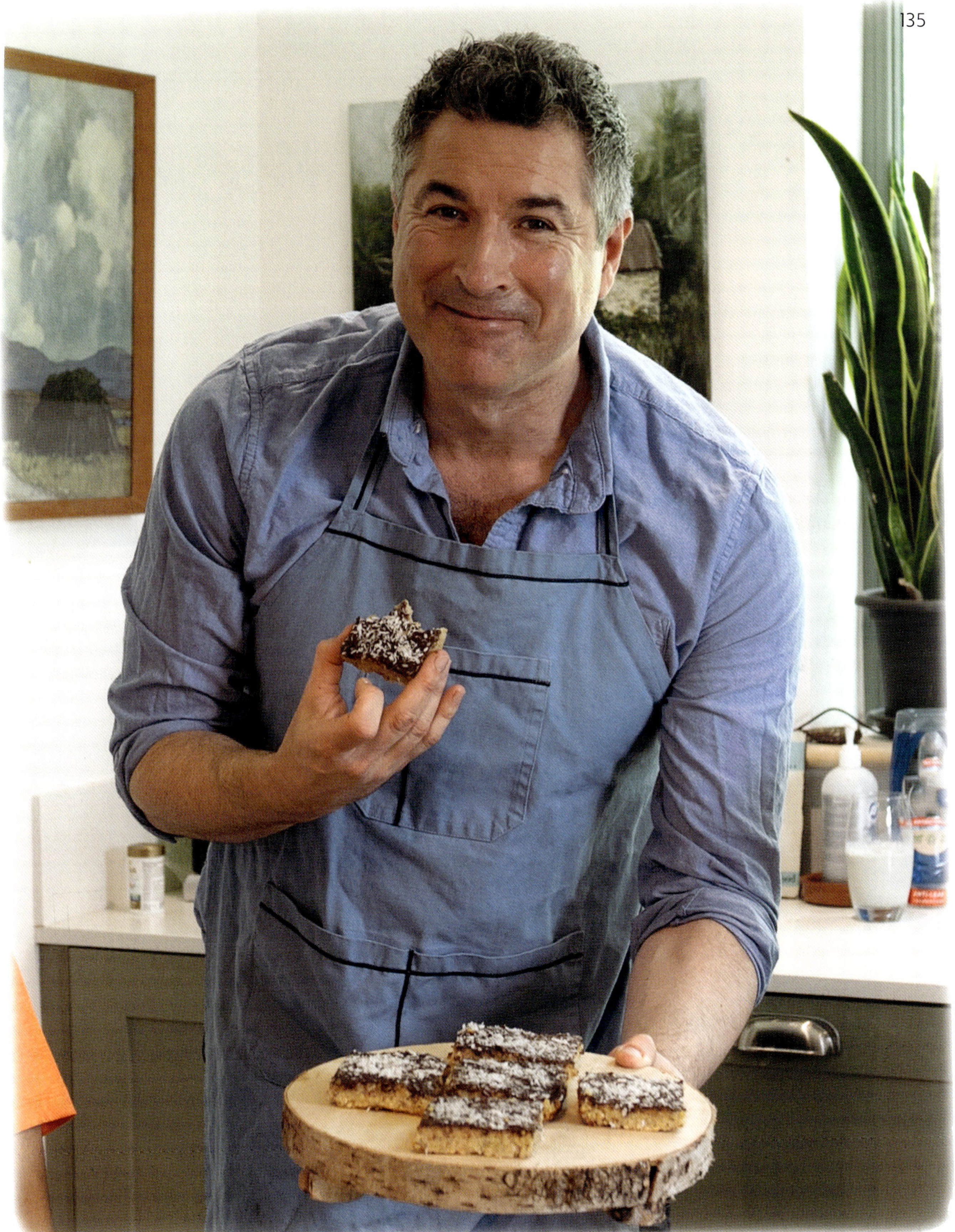

Acknowledgements

Firstly, thank you for buying this cookbook, I hope you enjoy the journey of creating nourishing recipes.

I would like to thank my friend, inspiration and mentor Cheryl Thallon for believing in me with the initial idea of this cookbook which has been a lifelong dream and now a dream come true, thank you Cheryl! I would like to pay a special tribute to Cheryl's husband Shaun who was always so kind and supportive with his words of wisdom anytime we would meet altogether in Ireland and the UK, thank you Shaun!

Special thanks to my wonderful loving husband Niall, my pillar of strength and the creative food stylist for this book, also our adopted French Bulldog Leon who brings me on walks of inspiration and clarity. My close friends Michael Holden, Eddie Fox, Rachel Henderson, Suzanne Doyle, Mary Darby Byrne, Suzan Turan, Claudia Stokes O'Dwyer, Michelle Walsh, Drew Young, Jennifer Kavanagh, Kate Bentley and Mel Keane. Also, my caring colleagues Fiona Mullen, Padraig Hyland, Alan McGrath, Eamon O'Sullivan, Joe Dalton, Jane Irwin Smith, Cathy Doyle, Hannah Dare and Rachel Dare. My nutrition and culinary mentors Richard Burton, Maggie Lynch and Carmel Somers whom have always guided me and pick up the phone for chats.

I'm so grateful to Joanna Clements and the wonderful supportive hardworking team at Suddenly Publishing & Viridian Nutrition for all their awe-inspiring creativity, editing, design and marketing input throughout this magical cookbook journey. A big thank you to the incredible authentic Mark McGuire at Big Adventure Media for his ongoing support and creative talent with the photography throughout the cookbook.

Behind the scenes Darren Farrell of Fitzgerald's Kitchens, Gary Hick of Rhatigan and Hick, Evan Doyle of Brook Lodge Macreddin Village, Maggie Roche and Paddy O'Toole of Ballybeg House, Philip Hadden and Rebecca Allen of Tinahely Farm Shop, and the Down to Earth independent health store.

Many thanks to all the fantastic recipes testers all over the country taking the time to create, cook, eat and have fun with all of the recipes plus more with honest feedback, especially - The Farrell family (Veronica, Alannah and Amelia), The Murdock family (Niamh, Elise and Ronan). My pal Andrea Rochford for organising the Harold recipe testers (Dwyer family, May family, Dolan family, McCann family and Connell family), Kathy Mullen, Ruth Barry and their phenomenal food styling 2nd year students of St Fintan's High School Sutton and Cathy Hyland Ryan and team at the Rotunda Maternity Hospital.

Thank you to all the independent health stores in the UK and Ireland for their ongoing care, empathy and love. And all involved with the independent food retail sector, stores, brands and customers.

Always I have my Mum and Dad in my heart and soul, Margaret and Paddy McCabe. I wouldn't be here today if not for the roots they planted for me to blossom in the independent health food sector. I'm so proud of my nephew and godson Padraig McCabe who assisted me with preparing recipes and his dedicated parents, my brother Brian and my sister in law Iris, thank you for all your support.

Lastly thank you to all the angels, guides, fairies and elements surrounding me every day minding me always, & thank you universe!

Oliver 😊

And to my supporting cast...

...please take a bow!

Further Resources

Healthy Does It

A great website to help you understand the natural products and healthy foods that might be right for you and where you can obtain them. You can also find a useful A-Z of nutrients and a resource hub for you to learn about all things natural health.

www.healthydoesit.org

Find a Health Store

Local health food stores are a one-stop shop for staple foods, nutritional supplements, and expert advice. This helpful store locator will help you find your nearest one.

www.findahealthstore.com

Health Stores Ireland

You can find a range of resources, news, and health advice on this website dedicated to health stores in Ireland.

www.irishhealthstores.com   HEALTH STORES IRELAND

Viridian Nutrition

Nutritionist-formulated supplements that are kind to your body and kind to the world. On the website you'll find nutrition advice and a variety of supplements, including a range designed especially for children.

www.viridian-nutrition.com   VIRIDIAN

Keep up-to-date with my events, news and latest recipes on my website:

www.olivermccabe.ie

Praise for Kids Kitchen Takeover

"Kids are our future! Inspiring children to take an interest in nutrition and deliciously tasting food is Oliver McCabe's mission in this excellent cookbook, essential for children, parents and families."

Patrick Holford
World-renowned nutritionist and author

"This is Super Stuff! We've known Oliver for many years. He really knows the health food world as he is a real health food ambassador."

Stephen Flynn
Global influencer, chef, author,
and co-founder of *The Happy Pear*

"The scrumptiousness of Oliver's recipes for kids is unstoppable benefitting not only kids' nourishment but also animals, human health and the earth."

Susan Hargreaves aka 'Veganza'
Author and founder of global vegan
animal welfare charity *Animal Hero Kids*

"With the ultra-processed food industry determined to get another generation hooked on nutritionally depleted food, children's health is under than threat more than at any time. Showing kids that it's fun and easy to cook delicious, healthy meals and snacks with fresh, plant-based ingredients is a great way to equip them with the life skills to help them live healthier, happier lives. Oliver McCabe's brilliant new book couldn't be timelier. Sure to inspire little foodies everywhere, it's the perfect addition for your kitchen book shelf."

Health Stores UK

"Oliver McCabe has a long association with Health Store Ireland, both as an active member and an ambassador for the sector. He has been valuable collaborator with many projects and events which are designed to make wholefoods more accessible and ultimately more convenient and tastier for the consumer. His good humour and quick wit compliment his deep knowledge of cookery, a passion for healthy eating and support of independent family run food retailers."

Health Stores Ireland

My Recipes

Recipe name

_____

Servings　　　　　　**Prep time**　　　　　　**Cooking time**　　　　　　**Temperature**

Ingredients　　　　　　　　　　　　　　　　**Instructions**

My Recipes

Recipe name

Servings   **Prep time**   **Cooking time**   **Temperature**

Ingredients   **Instructions**

My Recipes

Recipe name

Servings　　　　**Prep time**　　　　**Cooking time**　　　　**Temperature**

Ingredients　　　　　　　　　　　　**Instructions**

My Recipes

Recipe name

___

Servings   **Prep time**   **Cooking time**   **Temperature**

Ingredients   **Instructions**

My Notes

My Notes